Contents

PR IN PRACTICE SERIES

Public Relations Strategy

Sandra Oliver

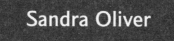

CHARTERED INSTITUTE OF PUBLIC RELATIONS

KOGAN
PAGE

London and Philadelphia

First published in 2001 by Kogan Page Limited
Second edition 2007

120 Pentonville Road
London N1 9JN
United Kingdom
www.kogan-page.co.uk

525 South 4th Street, #241
Philadelphia PA 19147
USA

© Sandra Oliver, 2001, 2007

ISBN-10   0 7494 4865 2
ISBN-13   978 0 7494 4865 3

British Library Cataloguing-in-Publication Data

A CIP record for this book is available from the British Library.

Library of Congress Cataloging-in-Publication Data

Oliver, Sandra.
    Public relations strategy : a managerial approach / Sandra Oliver. – 2nd ed.
        p. cm.
    Includes bibliographical references and index.
    ISBN-13: 978-0-7494-4865-3
    ISBN-10: 0-7494-4865-2
1. Public relations–Management. I. Title.
    HD59.O45 2007
    659.2–dc22
                                                                2006034169

Typeset by JS Typesetting Ltd, Porthcawl, Mid Glamorgan
Printed and bound in Great Britain by Creative Print and Design (Wales), Ebbw Vale

List of figures and tables

FIGURES

TABLES

Foreword

All the indications are that public relations is being taken more and more seriously by senior managers in large and small organizations. The number of public relations' professionals occupying board level positions is increasing, every FTSE company now has a public relations department and central government, post the Phillis Review of 2004, has invested heavily in training and development for civil servants who work in communication roles. Salaries for senior professionals are increasing and there are plenty of jobs for those who are able to operate comfortably and competently at C suite level.

This book provides an overview of the strategic role that public relations can play.

It points to the main reasons why it should be regarded as a core function in the organization's strategic armoury and how it fulfils that function. Dr Sandra Oliver explains how public relations can contribute to the fundamental systems in organizations and to support her arguments, provides an impressive raft of management theories that public relations draws on or relates to.

She goes on to demonstrate the central role of public relations in governance, reputation management, employee relations, sales and marketing and media relations. These are all aspects of organizational life that build the intangible asset base and make a critical contribution to overall prosperity and value – and that can be translated into hard cash. In a knowledge based economy, the intangible asset worth of a company is often of a much higher value than its tangible assets and the province of public relations is to nurture and promote these intangible assets logically, therefore.

Dr Oliver also makes a valued contribution in explaining how public relations can be evaluated at a strategic level and its ethical dimensions.

The book is not intended to provide a detailed account of how these contributions are operationalized, that is done in other books in this series, but the case studies included illustrate how public relations has made a significant difference in areas of strategic importance to companies. This book gives the 'helicopter view' of public relations and as such will help practitioners set their own work in the wider organizational context and provide a glimpse of what public relations can contribute at the strategic level.

Anne Gregory
Series Editor

Preface

This book offers a glimpse into the proliferation of strategic management theories and models that have emerged to underpin public relations strategy in the last few years of e-commerce and the internet. Global expansion for industry and commerce has not only brought public relations management into sharp focus again but is clarifying context and status relative to other corporate priorities at any given time.

At the practical level, most in-house specialists are aware that they can carry out the tactical requirements demanded of them, such as media relations, trade shows and publicity events, internal and external publication production, including video, audio and film production, the annual report and other activities. Yet many struggle with main board directorates who, singly or collectively, ask questions that assume knowledge and appreciation of business strategy before appropriate responses are given and corporate public relations decisions made.

There is currently a fairly intense discussion taking place about the nature versus the nurture of strategic public relations particularly in respect of business and government communication versus propaganda, often referred to by the media as 'spin'. This puts added pressure on the public relations profession and the specialists who operate within it. However, all vocational disciplines have a private and public face to them and public relations, pivotal to corporate strategy, is no exception. Like management itself, the practice of strategic public relations is an art rather than a science. One thing is certain: e-commerce and the world wide web have changed not only the nature of a century's accumulated public relations theory and empirically based practice, but also the nurturing necessary for the next generation of managing practitioners, whether in-house (internal) or outsourced (external).

The global public relations industry is at a juncture of change and development where there is much confusion about the behavioural boundaries associated with its activities. While the academic subject of public relations is generally understood to be a management discipline for study purposes, many university departments around the world choose either not to identify with it as such or relegate it to being a subsidiary component of marketing, film or media studies. Of course, higher education generally is having to adapt to the information age and the complexities that this brings to all such interdisciplinary and multidisciplinary subjects, so to some extent the knowledge era offers new opportunities.

One issue that used to tax the minds of academics was that of public relations' comparability to other vocational disciplines such as accountancy or law in terms of its literature base and growing body of knowledge. Now, universities have clear pathways with prescribed indicators to measure attainment of public relations education (knowledge) and training (skill) at each stage of the professional development process until specified learning outcomes are demonstrably achieved and any Chartered Institute of Public Relations (CIPR) accredited award given. In the acquisition of public relations management competencies, it is understood that today's students have proven conceptual understanding and tactical ability at both strategic and operational levels.

As a text claiming to represent a brief overview of public relations at advanced strategic level, it ought, by definition, to be able to assume that fundamental management concepts and mechanisms are understood and need not be reiterated. Students of public relations, for example, proceed from the CIPR Foundation Diploma level before attempting the qualifying CIPR Diploma, some of which concentrates on public relations strategy. New publications such as *PR Business* are emerging to meet a need, but often the best public relations students from both profit and not-for-profit organizations are those with a management background or those prepared to struggle with the prolificacy of management texts and viewpoints.

How far techniques can be included in any book on strategic public relations management raises some interesting questions about critical analysis, not least the negative perceptions of public relations as mere opportunism or publicity stunts. This book includes cases to assess tactics through discussion of real world campaign summaries provided at the end of each chapter. The campaigns have all been IPRA Golden World Award category winners, and the outlines provided aim to provoke deeper reflection by readers, students and managing practitioners alike. Typical issues for discussion might include:

- key links between the chapter (theory) and the campaign (practice);
- any changes necessary to the campaigns to ensure 'best practice';
- what omissions appear to be revealed by the campaign narratives provided;
- what future research the campaigns point a need for in 21st century public relations;
- within the bounds of the information provided, whether evaluation criteria measure up empirically for quality assurance purposes;
- the way short-term event campaign results can stabilize/destabilize longer-term strategic planning cycles via their impact on other stake-holder groups;
- how any immediate beneficial outcomes should be managed for reputation and its ongoing sustainability.

Thus the book begins by introducing readers to my framework illustrating how the profession is organized through the expert functional activities that make up each of eight specialist strategic areas. Some areas, such as events management, increasingly operate autonomously, albeit not always to CIPR regulatory standards, such is the proliferating demand for such services. This is a challenge for the public relations profession, which may increasingly find itself required to expand its enforcement role to retain public confidence and respect. As a consequence, this revised edition ends with two additional chapters: Research Methods and The Ethical Dimension. They endorse the need for sound judgement at all times and the wherewithal to challenge everything we hear, see, say and do through the art of excellent communication.

Sandra Oliver
London, UK

Acknowledgements

I am grateful for permission to reproduce copyright material and all contributions are credited at source within the text. However, while every effort has been made to trace the owners of all copyright material, we offer apologies to any copyright holder whose rights may have unwittingly been infringed and welcome information that would enable us to contact them.

Special mention and grateful thanks must go to the companies featured in the updating of their material since the first edition in 2001; to the CIPR series editors for helpful comments; to Kogan Page for their support and translations of both editions; to member colleagues on the IPRA Golden World Award judging panel for their permission to include winning campaign entries; to my postgraduate students from around the world studying on the Thames Valley University (TVU, London) MSc Corporate Communication course, especially for the ever stimulating seminar debates; to that programme's Practitioner Panel whose professional input is always invaluable; to TVU, London's UK student associates and tutors working together on the CIPR qualifying membership diploma programme; to the worldwide family of pure and applied researchers who attend the annual US/UK Corporate Communication Conference sponsored jointly by the *Corporate Communication International Journal* and the Corporate Communication Institute; and to all the authors and analysts who have contributed and continue to contribute to the success of that leading academic research journal.

Special thanks go Jenny Johns; also to Lydia Abele, Clare Cochrane, Sarah Edwards, Paula Fernandez, Christina Genest, Michael Goodman, Peter Hill, Anna Leatham, Sandra Macleod, Fehmida Mohamedali, Ian Somerville, Giuliana Taborelli, Kanwal Virdee, Reginald Watts and all friends and colleagues whose belief in the power and influence of sound communication to make a difference to the greater good – and development of the public relations industry itself – never fails to encourage and inspire.

Sandra Oliver
London, UK

1

Not 'just' public relations: PR strategy in a management context

When the Chartered Institute of Public Relations produced the results of its Delphi Survey a decade ago, the need for definition of the term 'public relations' (PR) was second to the measurement and evaluation of public relations in a hierarchy of research requirements as articulated by Institute members, both academic and practitioner. With any developing profession, reliable and valid research brings it to maturity. However, if definition is still a problem, theories, models, techniques and strategies remain abstract concepts. Or do they? Who can clearly define all types of accountancy, medicine or law in a single definitive statement?

Many organizations, though, are making a move away from the term 'public relations' towards 'corporate communication management' in the naming of their restructured public relations and public affairs departments. Like the term 'management', public relations may rely more for its meaning when things go wrong than when things go right. Practitioners are well aware of the function of public relations and the techniques applied to carry out its commercial role in a business context. This chapter demonstrates how strategic public relations aligns itself to corporate strategy by involving an organization's full range of stakeholders. Before addressing this aspect, however, it is necessary to define what is meant by strategy.

WHAT IS STRATEGY?

Over a decade ago J L Thompson (1995) defined strategy as a means to an end when he wrote, 'The ends concern the purposes and objectives of the organization. There is a broad strategy for the whole organization and a competitive strategy for each activity. Functional strategies contribute directly to competitive strategies.' Bennett (1996) described strategy as 'the direction that the organization chooses to follow in order to fulfil its mission'.

However, globalization has changed the face of managerial texts on the subject. Mintzberg *et al* (1998) offered five uses of the word strategy:

1. A plan as a consciously intended course of action.
2. A ploy as a specific manoeuvre intended to outwit an opponent or competitors.
3. A pattern representing a stream of actions.
4. A position as a means of locating an organization in an environment.
5. A perspective as an integrated way of perceiving the world.

Australian author Colin White (2004) offered a broad cognitive map by suggesting that three elements are prescriptive, namely strategy as design, planning and positioning, while 11 others describe what actually happens in strategy making. These become strategy as:

● entrepreneurship;
● the reflection of an organized culture or social web;
● a political process;
● a learning process;
● an episodic or transformative process;
● an expression of cognitive psychology;
● consisting in rhetoric or a language game;
● a reactive adaptation to environmental circumstances;
● an expression of ethics or as moral philosophy;
● the systematic application of rationality; and
● the use of simple rules.

White recognizes the central role that communication with stakeholders plays in strategic thinking and operations management. Today's generic models of strategy highlight four approaches:

1. classical (analyse, plan and command);
2. evolutionary (keeping costs low and options open);
3. processual (playing by the local rules);
4. systemic.

These all shadow the history of public relations (see also p 8), from classical through evolutionary and processual to the systemic model espoused in this book and others. These four dimensions include variables of power and culture, which many of the traditional models lacked. Inevitably, this is important in assessing the nature of organizational reality. For example, there would be a different emphasis on an organization driven by its investment stakeholders such as financiers, compared with an organization driven more by the community and local government or customers and suppliers.

The reflective in-house public relations practitioner does this in the normal course of his or her professional control activity and will be aware that:

● major public relations decisions influence organizational aims and objectives over time;
● public relations decisions involve a major commitment of resources;
● public relations decisions involve complex situations at corporate, business unit or other stakeholder levels which may affect or be affected by many parts of the organization; and
● executive public relations decisions are inevitably based on best available intelligence and sound knowledge management at the time and outcomes are transmuted into the longer-term decision-making cycle.

Although it differs from organization to organization, it is common practice for strategy making to take place at three levels, the macro or corporate, the micro or business unit and the individual/team or operational level. In small to medium sized enterprises (SMEs), the business unit often operates at corporate level, whereas in the public sector, the UK's National Health Service (NHS) for example, strategic decisions are made from central government downwards, with operational strategies rolled out at local and regional level.

Whatever the structure, processes must be coherent and so communication strategies between various levels have to be consistent. There is often a lack of recognition of strategic decisions being made at different levels so the role of the public relations specialist is to ensure that consistency applies throughout, what UK politician Peter Mandelson referred to as being 'on message'. This did not mean 'common' or 'the same', although perception of the phrase was consistently changed by journalists and ministerial rivals to suggest that it did mean that. A basic understanding of managerial systems theory is crucial to all practitioners but, generally, the most pertinent theories used in public relations management can be summarized as follows.

Theories of relationships

- Systems theory which evaluates relationships and structure as they relate to the whole.
- Situational theory whereby situations define relationships.
- Approaches to conflict resolution which includes separating people from the problem; focusing on interests, not positions; inventing options for mutual gain; and insisting on objective criteria.

Theories of cognition and behaviour

- Action assembly theory is an aid to understanding behaviour by understanding how people think.
- Social exchange theory aims to predict behaviour of groups and individuals based on perceived rewards and costs.
- Diffusion theory whereby people adopt an important idea or innovation after going through five discrete steps: awareness, interest, evaluation, trial and adoption.
- Social learning theory whereby people use information processing to explain and predict behaviour.
- An elaborated likelihood model which suggests that decision making is influenced through repetition, rewards and credible spokespersons.

Theories of mass communication

- Uses and gratification – people are active users of media and select media based on their gratification for them.
- Agenda-setting theory – suggests that media content that people read, see and listen to sets the agenda for society's discussion and interaction.

Probably the most common area of confusion by practitioners in respect of these theories is in the day-to-day management of brand image. Corporate brand image is as important as product brand image. Indeed, marketing uses many of the same channels of communication as those used in classical public relations and often the same media too. Both product branding and corporate image branding are concerned to move audiences from awareness to clearly defined perceptions that are seen to offer competitive or social advantage, but the underlying psychological tools and techniques will be different and subject to stakeholder analysis.

POWER AND INFLUENCE

Because of its alignment with corporate strategy, strategic public relations incorporates power control models operating at the macro and micro levels, based around typical symmetrical models.

Most in-house practitioners know from experience that as advisers they rarely make final strategic business decisions or choices. This is usually made by the dominant coalition and thus, although all these factors may influence the choice of a model of strategic public relations, power control theory from organizational behaviour shows that the people who have power in an organization may choose the type of public relations programmes that they do for reasons best known to them. The traditional view of the in-house practitioner having a board appointment in order to better influence board decision making is only sustainable if the practitioner is highly skilled and experienced in environmental business management, organizational behaviour and interactive communication.

PUBLIC RELATIONS AND ORGANIZATIONAL CULTURE

Organizational culture is created by the dominant coalition, especially by the founder or CEO of an organization, and public relations managers do not gain influence if their values and ideology differ substantially from that of the organization. Organizational culture is also affected by the larger societal culture and by the environment. It affects public relations in the long term by moulding the world view of the public relations function and thus influences the choice of a model of public relations within an organization.

While such a model identifies many of the variables essential to communication management and control, it also shows that if a culture is essentially hierarchical, authoritarian and reactive, the dominant coalition will generally choose an asymmetrical model of public relations. Furthermore, it will choose not to be counselled by the public relations expert who traditionally was often not seen as having enough strategic

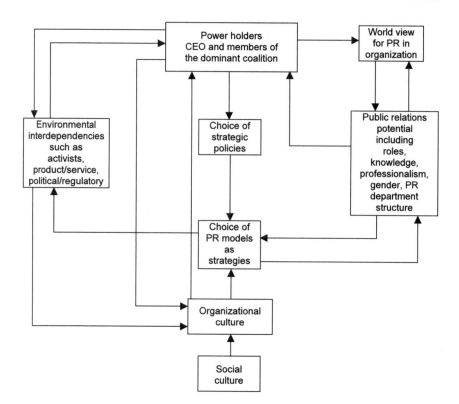

Figure 1.1 *Factors influencing choice of model*

Source: Grunig ed (1992)

Key
The box labelled 'World view for PR in organization' assumes that public relations is dominant in an organization but, as the arrows show, the world view for public relations is, 'a product of the world view of the dominant coalition, the potential of the public relations department and the culture of the organization' (Grunig, 1992, p 24). The arrow from environmental interdependencies to power holders indicates that, 'managers gain power when they have knowledge and skills that help organizations manage crucial environmental interdependencies'. The arrow from power holders to environmental interdependencies indicates that, 'the environment is in part at least the subjective perception of the dominant coalition'. The arrow from the choice of public relations models as strategies to the environment, 'depicts the critical relationship between strategic management of public relations and organizational effectiveness'. The final two boxes, 'depict the relationship among societal culture, organizational culture and excellence in public relations'.

awareness and therefore was of limited value. Many companies have changed their departmental names from 'public relations' to 'corporate communication' to reflect this development. With the future unknown, developmental debates centre on the dominant theoretical models I have identified; see Table 1.1.

BEST PRACTICE

Key day-to-day executive skills and technical expertise come together in professional practice to support public relations strategy in-house or outsourced to blue chip management consultancies and public relations agencies. In my eight-factor PR integration model shown in Figure 1.2, professional expertise is organized at micro (in-house relations) and macro (external relations) levels. Integrated communication tools and techniques can be broadly classified into eight strategic areas forming an integrated communication network. These have been defined as having a significant body of peer-reviewed knowledge underpinning them, based on academic theory and empirical research.

CORPORATE COMMUNICATION ACADEMIC MODELS

The study of corporate communication makes corporate communication perhaps one of the broadest multi-disciplinary and inter-disciplinary subjects available in universities today. Topics will be studied from:

- politics;
- economics;
- philosophy;
- languages, semiology and semantics;
- cultural studies;
- psychology;
- sociology;
- IT and computer studies;
- research methods;
- information studies including library/archival sourcing;
- journalism including technical writing;
- media studies including mass communication;
- advertising;
- marketing;
- business studies including transaction theory;

Table 1.1 *Dominant theoretical models*

Selected Characteristics	Dominant theoretical models		
	Classical PR	Professional PR	Corporate communication
Boundaries	Locus of control	Divergent	Convergent
Orientation	Greeks, Romans Pre-war USA	Post-war US/UK/Europe	Global
Ideology	Paternalistic	Collectivistic	Individualistic
Role	Public control	Systems management	Stakeholder relations
Relationship with main board	Administrative	Advisory/ executive	Strategic
Generic activity	Public affairs	Public relations	Divergent comm.
Status of workforce	Staff	Employees	Professional class
Relations with media	Social	Legal	Psychological
Role of institutes/ unions	Marginal	Adversarial	Collaborative
Change	Slow	Moderate	Continuous
Market position	Protected	Stable	Competitive
Attitude	Social stability	Essential Cost	Mutual dependence

Source: Oliver (2001)

- management studies including change strategies;
- entrepreneurship;
- human resource management including organizational behaviour;
- civil and industrial law; and
- ethics.

Universities still have difficulty in deciding whether to classify and invest in the study of this discipline as a 'media arts' subject area or a 'business and management' subject area. Media and creative arts faculty people approach public relations through journalism, film, radio and photography production (for events/publicity, etc) while business faculty people approach public relations through a management orientation based on planning and control in line with business strategy. Hands-on skills are learnt through workshops, sometimes provided by trainers/visitors, usually through the professional bodies such as the CIPR and IPRA, just as they are on continuous professional development (CPD) courses, in accountancy, marketing or IT through their relevant bodies. However, the methodological principles for development of public relations as an academic discipline are based on accepted research methods, albeit depending on the purpose of a particular piece of research or analysis, as shown in Table 1.2.

Three main areas of popular academic research continue to be:

1. business and political communication strategy, which includes public or government affairs and corporate reputation;
2. governance and leadership communication strategy, involving employees, managers, directors and shareholders; and
3. integrated marketing communication strategy.

As the three most research-based, they best support the public relations profession, both in Europe and the United States, at this stage in its history. The importance of the analytical approach for practitioners cannot be overestimated, given the critical role of monitoring and evaluation of campaign policy and planning in today's ever-changing multimedia, new technology context.

SEMANTICS

A long-standing CIPR definition of public relations is 'the planned and sustained effort to establish and maintain goodwill and mutual understanding between an organization and its publics'. Here, the definition implies strategic management by the inclusion of the words 'planned', and 'sustained', and the use of the word 'publics' for stakeholders, interested parties and other influential groups. A more recent CIPR approach is to refer to public relations as being 'about reputation – the result of what you do, what you say and what others say about you', and 'the discipline which looks after reputation – with the aim of earning understanding and support, and influencing opinion and behaviour'.

Alternative practitioner definitions nearly always identify a strategic role for public relations when they are heard saying that public relations is the management of all communication within the organization and between the organization and its outside audiences. The purpose is to create better

Table 1.2 *Key methods of data collection and methodological principles*

Method	Main purpose	Data collection	Sample	Analysis
Phenomenology Derived from philosophy	Study of the 'lived experience'	In-depth audiotaped interviews	Small purposive sample (usually between 6 and 20, though occasionally fewer), depending on the variety of experiences sampled	Exhaustive description; thematic analysis
Grounded theory Developed by sociologists to understand social issues	Generate theory from all available sources in a social setting	Semi-structured audiotaped interviews/focus groups, with or without observation/ documentary analysis	Usually between 20 and 40, but may be larger or smaller depending on the homogeneity of observations. Purposive sampling is followed by theoretical sampling until saturation of the data is achieved	Constant comparison – data analysis proceeds with data collection, sampling and development of the interview guide. Leads to emergent concepts and categories
Ethnography Developed within anthropology	Gain a perspective of a culture, for example an organizational setting	Participant observation including interviews with 'key informants'/ documentary sources field notes/video recording	Focuses on fieldwork with 'immersion' in the setting. Numbers not relevant	Thick description – describes detailed pattern of social interactions and meanings

	Description	Data collection	Participants	Analysis
Narrative analysis/ life history Based on biographical studies	Detailed study of people's lives and experiences, based on the stories they tell	Audiotaped unstructured interviews that encourage story-telling. Often last up to 3 hours	Few participants (often 6 to 10), often interviewed on more than one occasion	Narrative analysis – focuses on thematic content, structure and coherence
Discourse analysis From linguistic studies	Study of the ways that social realities and understandings are constructed through language	Audiotaped or videotaped conversations, often in naturalistic settings	May be as small as 2, as in a professional-patient interaction	Detailed interpretive analysis of text, with a focus on the use of language and verbal expression
Conversation analysis From ethno-methodology	Detailed study of 'tacit' means of communication	Non-participant videotaped observations of everyday activities	May be as small as 2, as in professional-patient interaction	Detailed analysis of non-verbal and verbal interaction, including turn-taking
Case study Management studies	Non-participant investigation using a variety of qualitative and quantitative research methods to investigate a 'case'. The case may be an individual, a group of people with a common area of concern, or an organizational unit or setting			
Action research	Similar to a case study, but the researcher is usually an active participant within the setting and may act as a change agent. The focus of investigation is determined with the work-based team, findings shared, change negotiated, results evaluated, and further areas of investigation jointly determined			

Source: Adapted from Walker *et al* (2005)

understanding of the organization among its audiences. Circumstances determine which audiences or sub-audiences are most important and need priority attention at any time.

Public relations practice involves management of an organization's reputation by identifying perceptions which are held of the organization and working to inform all relevant audiences about organizational performance. It is concerned with developing a deserved reputation for an organization, one which is based on solid performance not hollow hype. Reputation will not necessarily be favourable and may only be as favourable as the organization deserves. This becomes increasingly complex in the light of new technologies. Many CIPR members reject the notion of a change of name from 'public relations department' to 'corporate communication department' and argue that the impact of the internet on public relations is simply that it offers new electronic operational tools which don't alter essential practices. However, given that technology has so changed strategic operations for all forms of business and organizational communication, and given that human communication is the key measurable variable, the term 'corporate communication' better represents theory and practice of this discipline in large organizations.

Underpinning these changes and developments is the convergence of traditional telecommunications industries. 'Time-to-market' for some communications technology firms often narrowed from 20 years to six months during the 1990s. This convergence has led to some of the most lucrative consultancy in the corporate communication profession as industry tried to cope with the rapid rate of change in company and commercial cultures. Thus we see that corporate communication is both divergent and convergent in theory and practice, requiring special, advanced multi-skilling and powers of strategic thinking and operational practice.

While the public relations industry owes a debt of gratitude to the marketing industry for its development of numerous research tools and techniques, it has led to considerable semantic confusion. For example, one group of marketers defined public relations as 'building good relations with the company's various publics by obtaining favourable publicity, building up a good corporate image and handling or heading off unfavourable rumours, stories and events' (Kotler *et al*, 1999). Such academic marketers view public relations as a mass promotion technique and suggest that the old name for 'marketing public relations' was merely 'publicity', and 'seen simply as activities to promote a company or its products by planting news about it in media not paid for by the sponsor'.

Today, recognizing that public relations reaches beyond customers, the Chartered Institute of Marketing (CIM) concurs with the public relations industry that many of their tactics such as media relations, press relations and product publicity are derived from the public relations industry. From a strategic point of view, this is important in terms of quality assurance. In

global companies, a public relations or corporate communication department is never subjugated to the marketing department even though
marketing strategy may be linked to corporate business strategy, because
it fails to address the holistic links of strategic public relations with overall
corporate strategy (see Figure 5.1 on page 78). Strategy is essentially longer-
term planning while bottom line sales tactics, in spite of loyalty schemes,
often demand short-term, if not immediate, results. Of course both can
influence strategic decision making under changing circumstances.

Strategic public relations is concerned with managing the relationships
between an organization and a much wider variety of stakeholders or
audiences and range of priorities at any given time. The development
of macroeconomics and environmental management studies has put
pressure on the public relations industry to focus public relations strategy
on the dimension of the enterprise or organization which goes beyond the
bottom line of profit and shareholder price to include measures of corporate
success based on social accountability. As well as an organization's role in
the economic life of its country and its position in the global or national
marketplace, public relations counsel and activities form an important part
of an organization's policy in defining the environmental factors which
affect its corporate business activities. These include social stratification,
social welfare and national policy, technology, and the political, legal
and regulatory processes appropriate to a particular organization or the
industry in which it operates. All these factors need understanding of
attitudes and cultural norms that influence an organization's reputation
and public acceptability.

OPERATIONAL STRATEGY

Public relations is practised in organizations ranging from SMEs to transnational, multinational corporations with budgets bigger than many third
world governments. Baskin *et al* (1997) say:

> Public relations practitioners communicate with all relevant internal and
> external publics to develop positive relationships and to create consistency
> between organizational goals and societal expectations. Public relations
> practitioners develop, execute and evaluate organizational programmes
> that promote the exchange of influence and understanding among an organi-
> zation's constituent parts and publics.

Classical models of strategic management try to balance the internal
and external perspectives by correlating corporate mission with external
environmental factors over time. Adapting Pearce and Robinson (1982)
cited in Grunig (1992), the public relations operations manager must:

- communicate the mission of the company, including broad statements;
- develop a company profile that reflects its internal condition and capability;
- assess the company's external environment, in terms of both competitive and general contextual factors;

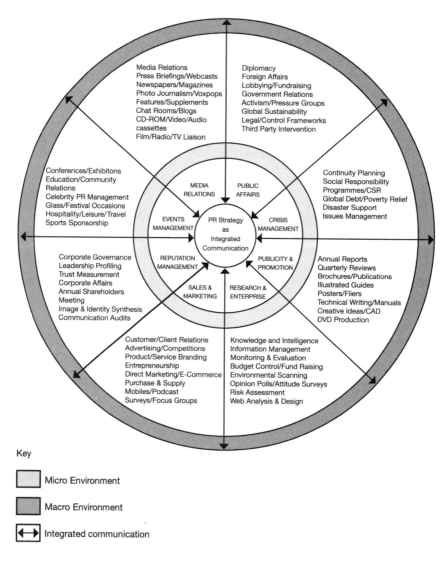

Key

☐ Micro Environment

▨ Macro Environment

[←→] Integrated communication

Figure 1.2 *The eight-factor PR integration model*

Source: Oliver (2006)

- analyse possible options uncovered in the matching of the company profile with the external environment;
- identify desired options uncovered when the set of possibilities is considered in light of the company mission;
- communicate to all prioritized stakeholder groups the long-term objectives and grand strategies needed to achieve the desired options;
- develop annual objectives and short-term strategies that are compatible with the long-term objectives and grand strategies;
- implement strategic choice decisions using budgeted resources by matching tasks, people, structures, technologies and reward systems;
- review and evaluate the success or otherwise of strategic campaign processes to serve as a basis of control and as benchmarks for future decision making; and
- incorporate ethical considerations into the decision-making cycle.

Inevitably, a crucial factor in such an exercise is relations with the media and identifying the purpose, nature and nurture required of any desired communication, as indicated by Grunig and Hunt's summary in Table 1.3. Grunig (1992) identified half of US companies as using the public information model, 20 per cent using the two-way asymmetric model and only 15 per cent using one or other of the press agency/publicity model or the two-way symmetric model. Of course, no one model is mutually exclusive and all four models may be applied within a single programme, not necessarily simultaneously but as appropriate for specific requirements. Grunig and his researchers at the IABC asserted that quality assurance is best achieved through the two-way symmetrical model, which relies heavily on the analysis of feedback.

However, before looking at the role of feedback in best practice, it is necessary to revisit the concept of stakeholder theory and the responsibilities an organization carries in respect of its dealings with different groups, as shown in Table 1.4.

The role of public opinion in the behaviour of organizations continues to increase via the internet and, while the public relations profession has always been aware of its obligations to all stakeholder groups, a global economy is making for increasingly onerous relations. Edward Bernays said in 1923 that 'it is in the creation of a public conscience that the counsel on public relations is destined, I believe, to fulfil its highest usefulness to the society in which we live'. The CIPR today endorses this thinking, over 80 years later, in its code of conduct, as does the IPRA.

It has already been stated that communicating consistently between stakeholders or audiences does not mean communicating the same message. Rather, a fundamental requirement in public relations is to develop a consistent corporate message (and tone) that appropriately reflects the organization in the way that the organization wishes to be reflected, even

Table 1.3 *Four traditional public relations models*

Characteristic	Model			
	Press agency/ publicity	*Public information*	*Two-way asymmetric*	*Two-way symmetric*
Purpose	Propaganda	Dissemination of information	Scientific persuasion	Mutual understanding
Nature of communication	One-way; complete truth not essential	One-way; truth important	Two-way; imbalanced effects	Two-way; balanced effects
Communication model	Source → Rec.	Source → Rec.	Source → Rec ← Feedback	Group → Group ←
Nature of research	Little; 'counting house'	Little; readability, readership	Formative; evaluative of attitudes	Formative; evaluative of understanding
Leading historical figures	P T Barnum	Ivy Lee	Edward L Bernays	Bernays, educators, professional leaders
Where practised today	Sports; theatre; product promotion	Government; non-profit associations; business	Competitive business; agencies	Regulated business; agencies

Source: Adapted from Grunig and Hunt (1984)

as events, crises and issues are occurring. At the same time, messages must be capable of being adapted creatively to be understood by the different audiences targeted.

Ind (1997) wrote:

> Communication strategies should always start from the need to have speci-
> fically and ideally quantifiable communication objectives. The over-arching
> goal should be to achieve a specific positioning that will transcend the
> objectives for different audiences. The positioning itself should be derived
> from analysis.

Ind also suggests that public relations functions are to increase awareness and improve favourability:

Table 1.4 *Stakeholders' responsibilities*

Stakeholders	Responsibilities	
1. Customers	Economic issues:	profitability competitive products survival of the company product quality
	Ethical issues:	honesty the best possible products and services satisfy customer needs
	Voluntary issues:	long-term business function development
2. Employees	Economic issues:	work and income
	Legal issues:	cooperation following the regulations in dismissal situations
	Ethical issues:	good working conditions stability and security developing possibilities honesty
	Voluntary issues:	education supporting activities and interests
3. Competitors	Ethical issues:	truthful information fair marketing and pricing practices no use of questionable practices consistency and stability playing the game by the rules
	Voluntary issues:	good relations cooperation in industry-related issues
4. Owners	Economic issues:	return on assets/investments securing investments maximizing cash flow solvency profits
	Ethical issues:	Adequate information

Table 1.4 *Stakeholders' responsibilities (continued)*

Stakeholders	Responsibilities	
5. Suppliers	Economic issues:	volumes profitability
	Ethical issues:	honesty
	Voluntary issues:	sustainable and reliable long-term relations
6. Community	Economic issues:	taxes employment
	Legal issues:	influence on trade balance
	Ethical issues:	following laws and regulations
	Voluntary issues:	behaving with integrity supporting local activities
7. Government	Economic issues:	taxes employment influence on trade balance
	Legal issues:	following laws and regulations
	Ethical issues:	behaving with integrity
	Voluntary issues:	supporting local activities
8. Financial groups	Economic issues:	profitability security of investment
	Ethical issues:	adequate information
9. The environment eg, pressure groups	Legal issues:	compliance with environmental regulations
	Ethical issues:	environmental friendliness protecting the environment product recycling
	Voluntary issues:	proactive environmental management
10. Old and new media eg, press, TV, web	Legal issues:	compliance with the law, eg invasion of privacy in celebrity PR
	General issues:	compliance with guidelines, codes of conduct and ethics statements
	Voluntary issues:	internal web pages and chat rooms

Source: Adapted from Aurila (1993), in Oliver (1997)

Public relations loses out to advertising in its controllability, but it has the advantage over advertising in its ability to communicate more complex messages and in its credibility. The press coverage achieved through media relations activity has the appearance of neutrality. Also the ability to target specific media and audiences is enhanced by the flexibility public relations offers. (p 80)

This requires that a public relations strategy has to consider the ways that all its activities can be integrated, and the most practical and definitive way currently is to base public relations programmes on audience or stakeholder analysis. Just as it is critical to understand the theory and practice of customer relations in order to sell anything, so it is critical to understand what the different audiences or stakeholders need to know, where they are coming from in response to a message or organization's reputation, so that the principles of mutual understanding, not necessarily agreement, can be applied. As Ind says:

a communication(s) strategy can then be evolved which specifies within an overall positioning the communication requirements for each specific audience. This should not encourage communication anarchy with messages to shareholders contradicting those to consumers, but relevance. Working from audiences inwards encourages an organization to think of its communication mechanisms appropriately.

THE FEEDBACK CYCLE

Given the close psychological connection between perception and communication, critical feedback data will include identifying the cyclical responses to a message from receivers over periods of time. The traditional emphasis on feedback as knowledge and intelligence is as important as ever, but is changing in scale as a result of computer-assisted software.

Webster's definition of 'feedback' is 'the return to the point of origin, evaluative or corrective action, about an action or a process'. What this means in operational public relations terms is that it is possible to provide computer-tabulated information for managers about a firm's stakeholder practices and behaviour. Because this information is based on day-to-day perceptions, it is a powerful tool for communication analysis, reflection and adjustment.

Feedback can be derived from two sources: those identified for a generic programme to help corporate communication managers focus on key behaviour of their audiences, and those identified on a custom basis where a number of activities or a particular group of stakeholders for the company are identified. Feedback questionnaires and reports usually cover two areas: frequency and importance. Frequency is the extent to which the corporate communication manager uses a particular activity as perceived by the group or behaviours being evaluated. Importance is the extent to which the corporate communication manager feels a particular activity, message or behaviour is important. A typical feedback report will cover a section-by-section summary giving specific scores for each activity and a listing of the 'top 10' activities in order of importance with scores for each.

Feedback provides three principal areas of application. First, it can be used in organizational surveys to determine the extent to which a company is following practices that reflect or help to change the organization's reputation or culture. Secondly, it can be used on a one-to-one counselling basis where the process provides bottom-up or lateral feedback to supplement the top-down view usually proposed in dealing with journalists and/or employees. Thirdly, it can be used as a basis for a highly focused continuous professional training and development where managers are helped to improve their communication performance in practice areas where deficiencies are evidenced.

A typical research plan would always take into account both positive and negative feedback in its research brief, the work plan, data collection, analysis and evaluation. Given that stakeholder groups and subgroups may have cultural differences of language, religion, values and attitudes, aesthetics, education and social organization, feedback and the analytical tools applied to them are a specialist public relations activity.

CONTROL VS CODEPENDENCY

Nowhere does the importance of feedback inform the public relations controller more than during a crisis, where the business continuity plan heavily depends on its quality control during and after a disaster. Taking control while being codependent during a crisis taxes the public relations skills of the most experienced practitioner. With the central command role of communication, he or she must manage the crisis centre overall in collaboration with other key personnel responsible for health and safety, HR, marketing and operations, as well as manage any number of media enquiries.

Luftman (2004) examined 245 companies with continuity plans and surveyed 350 business technology managers. Even allowing for multiple responses, he showed the significance of the PR role during a crisis, which I later developed in my action stations framework. The Luftman data, shown in Figure 1.3, was published in *Information Week*, with the public

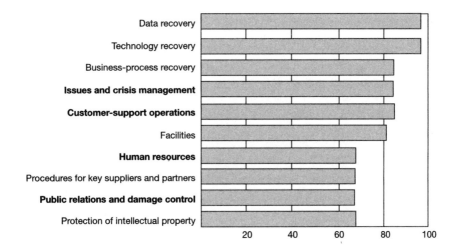

Figure 1.3   *Communication and the business continuity plan (BCP)*

Source: Luftman (2004)

relations roles emphasized to include human resources, because there would usually be much internal public relations activity during a crisis.

CAMPAIGN: PSA PEUGEOT CITROËN, SPAIN

This car company's campaign illustrates many of the key points raised in the chapter and shows how relations from organization, public and media perspectives were improved by a car firm after negative reactions to its expansion threatened its development.

PSA Peugeot Citroën's top plant is located in Vigo, Spain. However, there was a paucity of industrial space. Establishment of this plant changed it from a fishing village in 1958 to the current modern city. Demographic explosion converted Vigo into the region's industrial capital, where football is a favourite pastime. CELTA-Vigo, its club, became consolidated with PSA Peugeot Citroën sponsorship, but the relationship became estranged in 2003, when the club decided to expand its stadium located next door to the plant. The campaign had two objectives: to resolve a short-term threat and guarantee the plant's long term location.

Challenge vs opportunity

CELTA presented a project for the expansion of Balaídos Stadium in May 2003. Although the stadium is owned by the City Council, the club has a 100-year lease agreement for the site which not only houses the stadium but contemplates a future luxury hotel and shopping complex.

The project was a direct threat to the PSA Peugeot Citroën plant for motives related to space and an increase of traffic. The plant management informed the CELTA management and politicians in private that it was against the project. Despite this, CELTA went ahead and presented its project to the public, with a view to placing the club amongst the top names in Europe.

PSA Peugeot Citroën could be criticized by the citizens for subordinating life in the city to the company's activities. Proper management of the conflict could reinforce the tangible and intangible ties which link the company with its surroundings, so research and analysis revolved around three main areas.

Research

The three proposals for action were based on identification of similar cases where urban growth had resulted in the closure of an important industry; determination of how much the citizens of Vigo knew about the conflict between PSA Peugeot Citroën and CELTA; and definition of the values that underlay the society in Vigo which could affect future relations with the plant. A comparative analysis recommended the need for external allies: it noted that whenever other threatened industries opted for a head-on confrontation, it normally resulted in negative outcomes. Public opinion research monitored the conflict. Opinions were collected and contrasted, and decisions were implemented at various times over a number of weeks and analysed by a 'think tank'.

Strategic plan

The outcome was a strategy based on dismantling CELTA's project and ratifying a commitment to Vigo through actions that would help shape the city. Key audiences in the short term were to be the political parties' representatives in the City Council while the long-term target audience would be the voters.

The message conveyed was that PSA Peugeot Citroën supported the refurbishment of Balaídos (and not its expansion); was a world leader in spite of its limited space; was building Vigo on a day-to-day basis and shared its industrial culture with the city; and would not abandon Vigo unless forced to do so.

Local and regional media, as well as the different institutions present in the surrounding areas, were used to spread a first message. A second message was spread through sector and national media, with news coverage amplified by local media. Third and fourth messages were managed through the think tank. The latter's analysis of the future of Vigo and its conclusions, consistent with PSA's interests, were presented to the public.

Operational strategy

The plan was executed in three stages within specific time constraints.

Short term. After CELTA presented its expansion project to the public, the PSA Peugeot Citroën Vigo plant announced the production of the 7 millionth vehicle while the plant director stated: 'If Balaídos expands, PSA Peugeot Citroën will close down'. Influential city people were contacted privately to explain why expansion of the stadium would be negative and just days later, the media published opposition from unions, businessmen, politicians and citizens' groups to any project that threatened PSA Peugeot Citroën.

While third parties mustered opposition to the project, the plant organized actions geared towards promoting high production value, in spite of lack of industrial space and deficient infrastructures. A trip was organized for national media representatives to witness 'just in time' implementation of a car seat from drawing board to installation in the vehicle.

The specialized and economic press coverage next talked about 'the miracle of the automobile industry in Vigo'. Numerous press reports reached a climax with a report published in the daily newspaper *El País,* which has the highest circulation in Spain. Entitled 'rolling optimism' it focused on the merits achieved by PSA Peugeot Citroën in spite of threats such as the expansion of Balaídos.

Long term. In order to get citizen support to defend PSA's interests, public vision of the plant needed to be seen as a global reference point for the city and its citizens, beyond economic or industrial achievement alone.

Evaluation outcomes

The Balaídos stadium expansion project was rejected by the political parties that comprised Vigo City Council. On 1 July 2003, the municipal corporation signed an agreement committing itself to combat any project that could threaten the future of PSA Peugeot Citroën in Vigo.

Press coverage in the national media (both economic and sector) reinforced and expanded on the local and regional media coverage, on the importance of the PSA Peugeot Citroën plant in Vigo. This flow of media coverage resulted in an analysis by many public and private institutions of the automobile sector in Galicia and especially that of PSA Peugeot Citroën (eg, the 2004 GAXA report on the automobile industry – a reference for the sector, which paid special attention to the plant).

Lastly, the Ardora 2004 report (www.informeardora.com) was launched. The PSA Peugeot Citroën plant had achieved an unprecedented link with the city. The launch had united all of Vigo's conflicting parties, which resulted finally in *Faro de Vigo*, the principal local newspaper, stating: 'Passion for Vigo: Vigo is PSA Peugeot Citroën, PSA Peugeot Citroën is Vigo'.

REFLECTION

Based on the information provided:

i.   With reference to the broad theories of relationships described in the chapter, what type or types of relationship did Peugeot Citroën develop with its' three key stakeholder groups?

ii. What factors influenced the campaign strategy?

iii. How might the local decision outcomes impact on the company's global reputation?

iv. By applying the eight factor PR integration model, identify which technical activities contributed to the success of the campaign and thus which of the eight strategic areas took precedence.

v.   Using the BCP plan, suggest how the nature and quality of feedback will protect the organization from future threat.

2

PR's place on the board: a core governance role

Only 3 per cent of communication directors are currently on the main boards of UK companies and 23 per cent are on executive committees of FTSE-100 companies, according to research compiled by global public relations firm, Echo Research. However, the complexity of life in the 21st century is bringing public relations expertise back to the table, with a place on the main board in a joint governance role. After a decade or so of global criticism, industry and commerce are alert to the needs for joint steering. The public relations director is unlikely to be the CEO's favourite colleague and may frequently want to 'kill the messenger', but a competent CEO will trust both positive and negative counsel, so that advice is both respected and appropriately rewarded.

Organizations deal with pressures and developments from both internal and external drivers, usually concurrently, but previously it was often only in times of crisis that an organization valued public relations input. Most corporate decision making distinguishes between objective and subjective interpretation of events, takes a continuous view of change rather than reacting immediately to turbulent or sudden change, and approaches corporate strategy as a process involving choices rather than determinate positions. Managing public relations strategic decision making is no different and, like accounting or law, has its own body of knowledge, rules and regulations. However, it requires commitment from the CEO and main board members if the public relations director is to be able to fulfil his or her remit by applying such knowledge with the authority required.

Public relations advice has traditionally relied on case studies and empirical research to provide a base on which to draw and develop models of theory and best practice. Few practitioner writers adopt a polemical position about the communication aspects of public relations, yet, like most fledgling disciplines or professions, they are often criticized for being too descriptive and banal. An upsurge in the number of public relations research consultancies and an increase in client billings are an indication of recognition of the need for proven expertise.

TOP-DOWN, BOTTOM-UP COMMUNICATION

The CEO will want to extract value for money and insist on measured justification for public relations expenditure, but a strong, transformational leader will recognize the dangers inherent in not having expert public relations communication input at board meetings. Canadian writer Gareth Morgan looked at management performance and there is not one of his nine leadership competence modes in which communication does not play a central operational role; see Table 2.1.

It has been reported that CEOs spend between 50 and 80 per cent of their working hours on average on communicating with stakeholders of one sort or another, which suggests that they not only develop strategy but must be seen to operationalize it through the key competency of communication and concomitant public relations, although it is rarely identified see the first mention in Table 2.2.

Generally referred to as 'environmental scanning', the public relations specialist will investigate and analyse internal and external pressures, diagnose problems confronting the organization, suggest future trends and developments, and propose or counsel prescriptions for future action and, in the case of crisis management, remedial action. To analyse the pressures and problems confronting the employing organization or company, then it is understood that a number of proactive public relations processes are needed. These include using a variety of methods for collating public relations data such as:

- electronic sources such as CD-ROM library indexes and other organizational sources and external reference materials;
- different interpretations of the public relations problem which incorporate perceptions of target audiences, including the media;

- the extent to which it is possible to define and predict future trends;
- the contribution of managers and employees as a resource in meeting the public relations campaign or corporate communication objectives.

Table 2.1 *Communication in leadership*

Cultural model	Communication/PR Model
<ul><li>Reading the environment</li><li>Proactive management</li><li>Leadership and vision</li><li>Human resource management</li><li>Promoting creativity, learning and information</li><li>Skills of remote management</li><li>Using information technology</li><li>Managing complexity</li><li>Developing contextual competencies</li></ul>	<ul><li>Environmental scanning (external forces), issues management, planning, monitoring and evaluation</li><li>Mission/intelligence data</li><li>Relationship building/perception</li><li>Adaptive/interpretive strategies</li><li>Media relations, lobbying</li><li>Interdisciplinary nature of PR/crisis management</li><li>A management discipline involving a wide variety of stakeholder relations</li></ul>

Source: Oliver (2001), based on Morgan (1997)

Table 2.2 *Importance Of Global Leadership Compared With Other Needs (Based On A Survey Of US* Fortune *500 Firms)*

Dimension	Average rating
Competent global leaders	6.1
Adequate financial resources	5.9
Improved international communication technology	5.1
Higher quality local national workforce	5.0
Greater political stability in developing countries	4.7
Greater national government support of trade	4.5
Lower tariff/trade restrictions in other countries	4.4

1 = Not at all important; 7 = Extremely important

Source: Gregerson *et al* (1999)

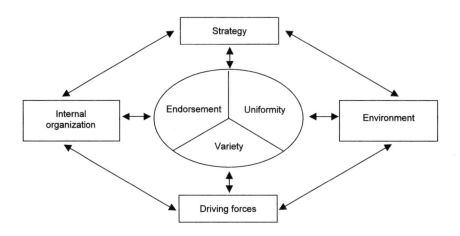

Figure 2.1   *Factors in the choice of communication policy*

Source: Van Riel (1995)

Van Riel's model shown in Figure 2.1 gives the strategic public relations director a focus for choosing a particular type of communication policy, by analysing the firm's corporate strategy in relation to the similarity or otherwise of the driving forces affecting the firm's mission, the amount or nature of control exercised by the board directors and the scale of environmental pressure on the organization. The communication policy is then derived from measures of endorsement, uniformity and variety.

One of the criticisms of the corporate strategy literature is that it rarely makes a distinction between different organizations in terms of their ownership, organizational size and mission. Clearly, private companies, voluntary bodies and public services adopt different approaches to their organization and objectives, but this is reflected more in the culture of each organization rather than in the process of communication. The fundamental nature of human communication may be universal but message style and delivery may change to best fit the culture in which it is being set.

FROM FUNCTION TO STRATEGY

To illustrate this point, perhaps the most notable strategic management model for communication purposes is the Johnson and Scholes model adapted here in Figure 2.2.

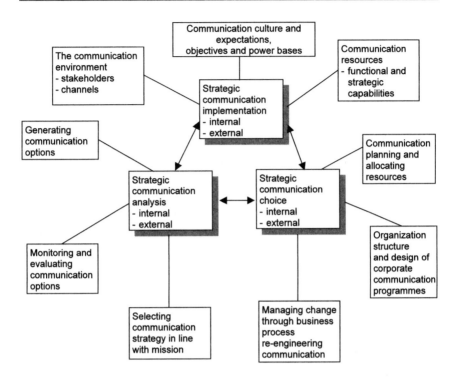

Figure 2.2 *Aligning communication leadership to corporate strategy*

Source: Oliver (1997), adapted from Johnson and Scholes (1993)

There are a number of weaknesses in this model, or at least potential for misunderstanding. While the model shows the essential elements of the strategy process, it is not linear, starting at the establishment of a mission and ending with implementation. As all competent public relations practitioners know, these processes must run in parallel and with consideration of resources and the practicalities of implementation. Johnson and Scholes attempt to discuss the process of managing strategically through human resources and make the reader more aware of the tactical requirements necessary for the strategy process to be effective. They include a model of stakeholder mapping to characterize stakeholders in terms of their level of power and interest in any outcome. They offer the model shown in Figure 2.3 as a useful analytical tool in assessing communication priorities at any given moment in time.

This approach suggests that, although mission statements articulate organizational objectives and these objectives are usually derived from economic managerial or social responsibility considerations, stakeholders

		Level of interest	
		Low	High
Power	Low	Minimal effort	Keep informed
	High	Keep satisfied	Keep players

Figure 2.3   *Stakeholder mapping matrix*

Source: Johnson and Scholes (2002)

have expectations which may not always be met. These expectations relate to the performance of the organization as well as being influenced by the external cultural context in which the organization is operating. Stakeholders have different degrees of power to determine the objectives of an organization and various levels of interest in exercising that power, and so stakeholder objectives affect the development of future organizational strategies.

Business re-engineering in the 1980s challenged firms to think more deeply about process. The systems approach to management is not just a process of analysis and reductionism but one of linking things together – the process of synthesis. In the 1990s, Johnson and Scholes produced a model for analysing organizational culture which they argued was essential if synthesis were to occur. They referred to the interplay of various factors in organizational culture as the cultural web or the mindset of an organization – that is to say, the way it sees itself and its environment. In Figure 2.4, they suggest formal and informal ways that organizational systems work through important relationships (structure); core groupings (power); measurement and rewind systems (control); behavioural norms (stories); training (rituals); language and livery (symbols); process and expected competencies (routine). There can only be synthesis if communication is performed to a high standard in linking together these strategic areas for competitive advantage.

On a more philosophical note, it is worth considering here how these factors make up a paradigm, as the organizational paradigm lies at the heart of any public relations change strategy. It describes a set of preconceptions

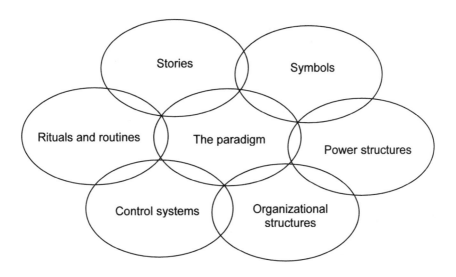

Figure 2.4 *The cultural web*

Source: Johnson and Scholes (2002)

which underlie people's way of looking at the world in general, not just an organization. It comprises a set of assumptions which people rarely question. From time to time a paradigm is shaken up and a paradigm shift takes place. In such an event, textbooks have to be rewritten as a paradigm shift involves the rethinking of basic assumptions underlying people's perceptions. Paradigm shifts, that is, fundamental changes in the ruling paradigm, are rarely dramatic in business and management, although electronic communications and global technology are accelerating change pertaining to the ruling paradigm of strategic public relations theory and practice.

Electronic systems and processes, particularly in respect of media relations, are working under an underlying set of assumptions and beliefs which are changing and undergoing a revolutionary paradigm shift as a result of cultural implications of globalization. At such times, organizations impose tighter controls. For instance, there are few organizations where managers are allowed to differ openly from or criticize the official line on strategy and policy, yet this may lie at the heart of the public relations expert counsel. Adherence to the accepted way of running an organization and the markets within which an organization is operating may not be openly criticized, and internal communication will attempt to reflect and reinforce the official line, through the company newsletter, for example.

COGNITIVE DISSONANCE: COPING
WITH CONFLICT

The Stacey (1991) approach to strategy takes conflicts inherent in any organizational processes resting on cultural differences and change and provides a model of *ordinary* and *extraordinary* management. Modern models of strategy formulation stress the instability of the relationship between an organization and its environment because time and dynamics never stand still. In any organization there is a perceived need to maintain stability and harmony while making sure that the organization can change in order to survive. This contradiction is expressed by Stacey as ordinary management on the one hand and extraordinary management on the other. These are useful concepts to critically appraise the role of public relations in corporate strategy. They reflect the fundamental philosophy of public relations in that the overall corporate message must be consistent (ordinary management) while monitoring changes in stakeholder perceptions that could impact on corporate objectives (extraordinary management) and which in turn lead to changes in the message.

The challenge for strategic public relations is to accept widely that, for efficient operation at any given time, it is necessary for an organization to have a clear sense of purpose and unity, but also a parallel culture in which it is possible to raise safely a variety of viewpoints to challenge complacency and ensure survival. Clinical psychology tells us that it is important that cognitive feedback loops operate in a positive manner so that perception and communication can be updated and clarified where appropriate. This is the basis of the symmetrical models promoted by Grunig (1992).

Public relations choices are on the basis of rational criteria, but this is only possible when there is agreement on what the business is all about and what kind of environment it has to cope with. Stacey argues that managers only operate within bounded rationality. The complexities of modern organizations mean that they have to adopt a pragmatic approach to decision making and accept that they cannot conceptualize or accommodate all possibilities. Bureaucratic procedures help to simplify the manager's task, providing rules and procedures for tackling many decisions. A hierarchical management structure ensures that difficult decisions can be made within the context of the prevailing ideology – the official line of the ruling coalition.

Ordinary PR management

This description of ordinary management is necessary to ensure that targets can be met and that the organization survives through rational processes. It presupposes a stable environment and can only be practised in contained change situations. It is not a negative concept given that it must be practised if an organization is to be able to control and deliver competitive advantage. It also implies that public relations, however, is conducted on the basis of asymmetrical communication in which the organization 'gets what it wants without changing its behaviour or without compromising' (Grunig and White, 1992).

The asymmetric nature of public relations means that the organization will find it difficult to adapt to a changing environment because it does not recognize that communication with the outside, as well as its own employees, must be a two-way process. Stacey's (1993, p 72) definition of extraordinary management states that it is:

> the use of intuitive, political, group learning modes of decision-making and self-organizing forms of control in open-ended change situations. It is the form of management that managers must use if they are to change strategic direction and innovate.

Extraordinary PR management

Despite the potential dangers for organizations remaining exclusively dedicated to ordinary management, a closer look at what is involved in extraordinary management will explain British reticence. Extraordinary management involves questioning and shattering paradigms and then creating new ones. It is a process which depends critically on contradiction and tension. The changing of paradigms is a revolutionary rather than an evolutionary process and cannot be intended by the organization. Stacey argues that both forms of management have to coexist if the organization is to evolve and survive a changing environment. An organization needs to provide a stable basis for meeting its short-term objectives and targets while at the same time providing a basis for transforming itself in the future to respond to changes in the environment.

Some organizations fail to recognize the need to allow for extraordinary management and instead rely on radical changes of CEOs, chief executives, consultants and other outside change agents who have little understanding of the nature of the problems within the organization. This is where the public relations consultant has to be particularly aware and cautious of the conflicting demands that may be put upon service provision. Many practitioners argue that they do what they're asked, no more no less, within the brief and the fee. In that they are professionally pragmatic. However, that approach may not be conducive to being consciously aware of where a particular service provision fits into the overall scheme of things. When monitoring and evaluating the wider environment, important elements are dependent on perception of how change in one area can impact on other areas or overall.

The implications of ordinary management for public relations are familiar through relationships with major stakeholders:

- *Shareholders* – the annual report is a regular calendar project. For most shareholders asymmetrical communication of results will tend to apply, whereas with major institutional shareholders self-interest will dictate a degree of symmetrical communication, and a genuine desire to listen to their concerns will be essential and generally implemented.
- *Customers* – the marketing and sales departments will tend to dominate in this aspect of the public relations role but, increasingly, symmetrical communication is being recognized as essential to obtain competitive advantage through so-called relationship marketing. A long-term two-way relationship may be established with customers to allow for feedback into marketing strategy. Grant and Schlesinger (1995) developed the concept of 'value exchange' in which a company optimizes the relationship between the financial investment a company makes in particular customer relationships and the return that customers generate by the specific way they choose to respond to the company's offering. For this, careful attention to the behaviour of customers is essential.
- *Employees* – the ruling coalition within the organization can of course use a wide range of channels to communicate with employees to achieve the aim or harmony, fit or convergence to a particular configuration and to ensure that they share the same mental models or paradigms. Posters that repeat the published mission statement, memos, messages contained in the actions of management relating to discipline suggestions and so on all contribute to an overall strategic process.

Implications of ordinary and extraordinary management

The implications of extraordinary management for public relations are significant. The need for extraordinary management in order for the organization to survive and flourish in an unstable environment has been emphasized, but control of the extraordinary process has to be achieved by informal organization of its activities. As the formal organization exists to protect the paradigm, the status quo, managers who wish to change the paradigm have to operate within an informal organization in informal groups which they organize themselves. These groups can cope with uncertainty and ambiguity, anathema to the formal bureaucracy, and tap each other's perceptions of what is going on in the organization.

According to Stacey, these groups are essentially political in nature. People handle conflicting interests through persuasion and negotiation, implicit bargaining of one person's contribution or interests for another's, and power exerted by means of influence rather than authority. This informal system has been referred to as 'the network system' and often lies at the heart of public relations expertise. These can coexist with hierarchy and bureaucracy, but must be encouraged by the actions of the bureaucracy and supported by top management.

When organizations manage successfully to combine ordinary with extraordinary management to create an innovative culture while maintaining stability, a sound public relations strategy plays a core role in sustaining the firm's corporate strategy. Both support competitive advantage while ensuring the capability to ward off hostile competition, pressure groups and media.

The concept of extraordinary management may lead to groups within the organization attempting to undermine the control of the organization and, ultimately, the ability of the organization to adapt requires that subversive activity takes place without control being lost. Decisions are not made by organizations as such, but rather by dominant coalitions within organizations, and these coalitions are not likely to be defined clearly in the official organization chart. White and Dozier (1992) argue that dominant coalitions still need information to help them make decisions. This is frequently provided by 'boundary spanners', that is individuals within the organization who frequently interact with the organization's environment and relay information to the dominant coalition.

THE CEO AS CULTURAL ICON

The strategic challenge for most organizations today is adapting their structures, processes and cultures to achieve sound relationships built on long-term mutual advantage through the integration of internal and external communication. The principles and communication processes of public relations contribute to all cultural aspects of an organization, with the CEO as the figurehead or cultural icon. They become a representative and leader of the organization's culture by his or her management style. Grunig *et al* were really discussing management style when they advocated symmetrical communication as best practice and, in today's language, the management style can often drive the corporate brand. As Ind writes:

> A corporate brand is more than just the outward manifestation of an organization, its name, logo, visual presentation. Rather it is the core of values that defines it... Communications must be based on substance. If they are not, inconsistency creeps in and confusion follows shortly thereafter...

What defines the corporation in comparison with the brand is the degree of complexity. It is larger, more diverse and has several audiences that it must interact with. The corporate brand must be able to meet the needs of the often competing claims of its stakeholders. To achieve that it must have clarity of vision, of values and of leadership. (1997 p 13)

The critical role of communication in operationalizing corporate mission and translating it into reality, and the importance of vision in the achievement of corporate objectives, are based on perception as a measurable variable of reality. Strategic planning models relate to public relations planning through open systems theory and general management tools such as hard line (not necessarily bottom line) value-added concepts. Many public relations professionals will argue that this is not new. Such factors have always existed as benchmarks for justifying their intangible but critical contribution. The difference today is that IT capability produces a variety of identifiable factors that can be seen to be part of an organization's intellectual capital, if not essential to its survival on occasions.

The public relations expert acts as specialist counsel to a corporate boardroom and his or her technical input is fundamental to management in sourcing, analysing, assessing, managing and tracking information and translating that information for the benefit of the corporate whole. Through flexibility and change, organizations today have to be lifelong learning organizations. They must encourage effective symmetrical communication to such an extent that external audiences such as media and dominant political coalitions can occasionally influence or even drive strategy from time to time without destabilizing it. An organization making policy in response to public criticism alone may prove to have revealed weak management based on poor strategic planning.

PERFORMANCE ASSESSMENT

Public relations strategy, like any other variable in corporate planning, must be able to identify measurable performance indicators. The eight-factor assessment shown in Figure 2.5 is a checklist, with each variable having its own tools and techniques in the short and longer-term operating schedules.

In monitoring and measuring performance, in-house or consultant public relations professionals act as boundary spanners by translating meaning from and about the organization in relation to the environment. They will counsel the CEO and top management about the organization's implicit assumptions. White and Dozier (1992) describe the case of a logging company which might view trees as a crop to be harvested rather than a natural resource to be cherished. Indeed, the logging company's

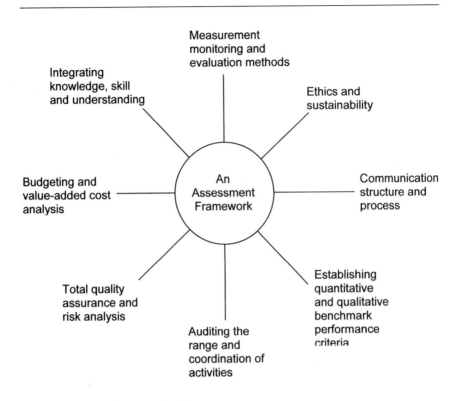

Figure 2.5 *Performance indicators*

Source: Oliver (1997, 2004)

traditional world view is embedded in its language as, for example, when it refers to 'timber strands', a term implying that trees are there to be harvested like 'strands' of corn. During a symmetrical communication process, conflict between an organization and environmental pressure groups can be forestalled if public relations professionals fulfil their role as boundary spanners by ensuring that there is a two-way exchange of information or perception between the organization, the groups involved and the wider, often media-led environment.

In another example, from local government, the dominant and ruling left-wing coalition within a UK local authority might have a world view which saw the town for which they are responsible as consisting of needy people with rights to subsidy and support. A different, say right-wing, group might view the situation as one consisting of local council taxpayers being burdened with payments and challenge money going to needy people who may be exempt from paying council tax. In this latter case, the public relations task would be to increase awareness and modify the unidimensional view of the dominant coalition while simultaneously communicating the needs of the poor to the ratepayers within the community without loss of coherence.

ASSESSING FUTURE PERFORMANCE

The public relations search for strategic factors in the environment cannot ignore the future, however difficult it is to assess. There are innumerable cases of organizations that failed to spot the changes looming ahead which either threatened them or which provided opportunities for development that were then lost to competitors.

McMaster (1996) said that the past is a poor basis for predicting the future, an aim which is in any case not attainable. What organizations can do is to see their future by examining the structure and process of the present. McMaster is stressing that, although it is impossible to predict future detail, the structure of any future is a set of relationships within a complex system which is constantly adapting. For example, relationships with technology and other forces are always affecting the environment within which the organization operates. The challenge of foresight is the 'vast space of possibility' and McMaster cites 3M's success in organizing for foresight. New products form a very high percentage of its product range at any one time. These products have arisen not only from individual acts of foresight but from an organizational design and management culture which continually encourages new product ideas. In other words, the organization is itself the source of invention.

Nevertheless, the starting point for the development of future strategy usually involves a systematic analysis of the organization's environment from a review of external factors. Popular models are based on PESTLE, the interaction between factors in politics, economics, society, technology, law and ecology. Such models are beginning to appear static, with a tendency to drive out more positive visions of what the future might hold for a particular organization, when people start to think creatively 'outside the box' through the drive and ambition of a transformational leader.

TANGIBLE AND INTANGIBLE ASSETS

Inevitably, any vision of the future depends on resources. The strategic importance of a focus on resources arises because, ultimately, profits can be seen as a return on the resources controlled and owned by the firm. However, resources are divided into tangible and intangible resources.

For each of these, there are usually key indicators, or a way of measuring their value. Public relations practitioners have often been caught in a mire of confusion in an attempt at offering hard measures for intangible outcomes. Intangible resources, which used not to appear on UK balance sheets, are difficult to value objectively, even when recognized as being of value, but the UK now supports the public relations industry with current statutory regulations which address this key element of worth.

REPUTATION VS THE OPERATING AND FINANCIAL REVIEW

The mandatory reporting of non-financial performance for large companies is an important development in the publication of industrial and commercial annual reports and accounts and therefore reputation.

Non-financial performance was largely perceived as an additional public relations exercise, but narrative reports on intangible assets as core communication factors are now recognized as important to tangible outcomes. The CIPR framework shown in Figure 2.6 offers a practical five-stage plan for preparing an operating and financial review (OFR) for the annual report.

The value of a recognized brand name which is held in good esteem may be unrecoverable once lost. Sometimes value can be inferred when an acquisition takes place, the difference between the book valuation and the purchase price being denoted confusingly as goodwill arising on acquisition.

The CIPR definition of public relations as the planned and sustained effort to establish and 'maintain goodwill' and mutual understanding between an organization and its publics is, though, rarely enough. Goodwill needs to be grounded and made concrete. It has to be measured and accounted for and thus we see the recent rise in research and evaluation of corporate identity image and reputation. Brooking's (1996) classification of resources breaks down intellectual capital into market assets, human-centred assets, infrastructure assets and intellectual property assets. On the other hand, Quinn *et al* (1996) see professional intellect as operating on four levels of cognitive knowledge, advanced know-how, systems understanding and self-motivated creativity, which they regard as the highest level of intellect reflecting motivation and adaptability. Petrash (1996) described the approach to intellectual capital management adopted by the Dow Chemical Company by defining intellectual capital as a formula:

Stage 1 Task Force	Stage 2 Stakeholder Audit	Stage 3 Benchmarking	Stage 4 Reporting Methods	Stage 5 Success Measurement

Stage 1 — Task Force

Board
Duty of the directors of qualifying companies is to produce an OFR: future plans, opportunities, risks and strategies

Key role for non-executive directors

Establish a Task Force to drive the OFR initiative

Task Force
Composition, corporate communications and other functional heads, non-executive directors, others who interface with stakeholders

Workshop to gain buy-in of Task Force members and key contribution

OFR Content and Process
Plan of OFR programme and responsibilities

Corporate success model (objectives, strategies, values etc.) as benchmark

Stage 2 — Stakeholder Audit

Task Force
Evaluation of stakeholder communication needs – internal and external including non-shareholders.

Prioritise audiences:

Primary	Secondary
Shareholders	Analysts
Investors	Media
Employees	Consumer organisations
Suppliers	Government/NGOs
Distributors	Regulators
Consumers	Trade unions
Communities	Potential customers
Pressure groups	

Stakeholder Audit – scope:
Research (existing/commissioned)
Focus groups/questionnaires
Anecdotal information
Findings and 'gaps'
Key issues
Risk assessment
Reconcile stakeholder differences

Results
Better understanding of how the company is perceived:
Awareness and perceptions
Reputation drivers
Relationships
Strengths and weaknesses
Communication effectiveness: messages & methods versus OFR criteria
Analysis
Action plan

Stage 3 — Benchmarking

Task Force
(plus optional external auditor)
Comparison of reporting practice with OFR criteria, with peer companies and against the company's own success model

Performance against OFR criteria

Compulsory	Yes/No
Statement of business	✓
Review of performance	✓
Prospects and impacts	✓

Material	
Management structure	✓
Shareholder returns	✓
Employment policies	✓
Environmental policies	✓
CSR policies	✓
Performance on employment, environment and CSR	✓
Reputation and other matters	✓

Comparison with industry indices (e.g. BiTC Corporate Responsibility Index) and own success model.
Environment, Workplace, Community, Marketplace

Results
(including stakeholder audit)
Steps needed to meet OFR criteria and front-end reporting best practice

Stage 4 — Reporting Methods

Task Force
Review effectiveness of stakeholder communication and the methods employed

Review
How could means of delivery and content be improved using OFR criteria and industry best-practice indices?

Report and accounts
Does it reflect the information needs highlighted in the stakeholder audit?
How does it compare with the best?
Does it satisfy OFR criteria?
Could front-end reporting be improved by dedicated section in the report and accounts or by separate reports?
Is the potential of the web being fully utilised?
Does the AGM need a re-think?
Is stakeholder communication 'joined-up' through formal and informal reporting?
Could public relations play a more effective oversight role?
Is the process independently audited?

Results
Reassurance that communications are stakeholder-driven and areas for improvement highlighted

Stage 5 — Success Measurement

Task Force
Implementation and monitoring for continuous improvement

Rolling monitor
Regular stakeholder audits provide rolling monitor of how well a company communicates the 'complete picture' – financial and non-financial
Publication of performance measures and indicators improves compatibility

Results
Greater understanding among stakeholders of financial and non-financial factors, their relationship and how they contribute to corporate reputation

The ingredients of the OFR

Draft OFR to Board

Figure 2.6 *An OFR matrix*

Source: CIPR (2002)

Key
Stage 1 Set up a cross-functional task force to head up the initiative, and carry out a review of the company's objectives and strategies to provide a 'success model' benchmark.

Stage 2 Identify stakeholders, internal as well as external. The OFR will broaden the role of the annual report and the range of stakeholders who will use it. Categorise audiences into primary and secondary. Conduct a stakeholder audit to discover what audiences know about the company, sources of information and nature of the relationship.

Stage 3 Compare the company's current reporting practice against OFR criteria, using a grid to identify information gaps, and against peer organisations via a range of available indices.

Stage 4 Review reporting methods and consider 'refreshing' reports, use of the web and format of the annual meeting.

Stage 5 Use the stakeholder audit as a rolling monitor of the effectiveness of non-financial reporting. The results of the methods used and outcomes should be published.

Intellectual capital = Human capital + Organizational capital + Customer capital

At the Dow Chemical Company they have over 75 multifunctional intellectual asset management teams which meet to review the patent portfolio. These are led by intellectual asset managers who in turn report to the intellectual management function. The whole is supported by an intellectual management centre which provides, for example, database support, career development of managers and sharing of best practice. What we are seeing then is a resource-driven approach to strategy based on the view that sustainable competitive advantage is derived from an identification of the firm's existing and future strategic capability. The long-term dynamic nature of a public relations strategy is that it is responsive to changes in the environment. It requires identification of existing and future communication gaps by sound professional public relations intellects, so that capability is underpinned by competence in the round.

STRATEGIC ALLIANCES

Managing the public relations activity surrounding the outcomes of strategic alliances has become an important financial option for organizations. They involve relationships between organizations which fall short of merger but which may go as far as mutual equity stakes, each organization owning a minority of shares in the other. On the other hand, they may involve no more than limited cooperation and consultation between otherwise bitter rivals but either way, the financial press will take a close interest. These alliances do not just involve very large organizations. No organization whatever its size can any longer hope to acquire all the skills and competencies necessary for operating in a global environment and it must therefore attempt to fill the gaps by working with other companies in partnership. The types of alliances that can arise are licences, joint ventures, franchising, private label agreements, buyer/seller arrangements or the forging of common standards and consortia. A prerequisite for a successful alliance is that there must be a clear purpose and objective for the arrangement and the process must be managed according to schedule and without loss of control. The role of the public relations strategist will be to ensure that media coverage does not give the organizations involved loss of control of their own destinies.

It would be interesting to see how long the strategic alliance approach lasts. For example, there are already claims that Japanese companies rarely commit their best scientists and engineers to projects sponsored by the Ministry of International Trade and Industry (MITI), while IBM set up a special facility in Japan where Fujitsu could test its new mainframe software before considering a licensing agreement. This provided some protection against loss of technological know-how through an alliance. Brouthers (1995) have a set of guidelines to be considered, namely complementary skills, cooperative cultures, compatible goals and commensurate levels of risk – what they call the Four Cs of successful international strategic alliances, as shown in the multinational giant, Philips' alliance network and current joint ventures (2006).

Figure 2.7 *Overview of Philips strategic alliances*

Strategy in its classical sense is a competitive model which aims to enhance the value of an organization to its shareholders. An organization chooses between strategic options, which may include mergers and divestments. Public relations strategists may be involved in merger acquisitions to increase shareholder value, merger acquisitions' decision-making processes, post-merger implementations and corporate divestment programmes. Once an organization becomes too unwieldy from a communication perspective, it will need to segment its image and identity. Philips has 10 key joint ventures and participations and has segmented them into three key activity sectors.

The trend for sustainability, if not a reversal of the movement towards growth, has led to the break-up of some corporations with the intention of releasing shareholder value. In a turbulent environment, organizations have to include in their range of strategic options a consideration of unexpected as well as planned research and development. This is often seen as a cost rather than an investment in the UK and, as with public relations programmes, there are disagreements about the extent to which expenditure should be subjected to vigorous cost-benefit analysis. Given the emphasis on producing downsized companies and outsourcing many essential functions, including public relations, issues around innovation and the virtual company, Chesborough and Teece (1996) assert, are on the increase in many companies.

CAMPAIGN: TAASA, USA

This campaign is an example of not-for-profit public relations activity requiring high degrees of political will, sensitivity and appropriate tools and techniques to achieve its statewide, strategic aim.

In April 2003, the Texas Association against Sexual Assault (TAASA) initiated a statewide public awareness campaign based upon the powerful true-life sexual assault stories of six Texas women. The campaign was a first for the state of Texas regarding the issue of sexual assault, and included paid as well as donated television and radio advertising, public service print advertising, media outreach, coalition building and grass roots efforts. The call to action was to encourage survivors of sexual assault to contact the toll-free sexual assault hotline or visit the TAASA website to get more information on sexual assault, to know they should 'Speak up. Speak out'.

Challenge vs opportunity

Every two minutes a person is raped in Texas. Two million Texans, or 13 per cent of the population, have been victims of sexual assault. For every report of sexual assault, there are four others that go unreported. Much confusion existed about what constitutes sexual assault, and more than half of Texas residents were not aware of sexual assault services available in their communities.

TAASA initiated a statewide public awareness campaign in 2003 to foster understanding and communication about sexual assault and to lift the social stigma associated with the issue. Research has been the foundation and guide for all aspects of the campaign's development. The 'Speak Up. Speak Out' campaign is the first time any state has undertaken public awareness efforts of this magnitude regarding sexual assault.

Research

Weber Shandwick and KRC Research conducted a statewide survey and coordinated focus groups to test Texans' true attitudes to sexual assault. This survey was the most comprehensive of its kind undertaken by a state to that date and revealed the startling results described above. TAASA also commissioned a sexual assault prevalence study conducted by the University of Texas and Texas A&M.

Strategic plan

Objectives were developed to

- create broad awareness of the issue of sexual assault throughout the state of Texas;
- increase understanding and knowledge of services available to prevent assault and support victims;
- position TAASA as a leading advocate and voice on the issue of sexual assault in Texas;
- develop a statewide public awareness campaign to educate the public on sexual assault;
- institute a paid advertising campaign across Texas to control messages to the target audience;
- provide TAASA executives to speak about sexual assault across the state;
- educate policymakers and gain legislative support of TAASA's agenda;
- conduct an aggressive community grass roots campaign disseminating information about community sexual assault services to hospitals, schools and law enforcement agencies and maintain regular communication; and
- educate Texas university students with specific college campus activities revolving around sexual assault.

Additional tasks were set to achieve the objectives, including:

- print coverage in TAASA key markets;
- broadcast publicity at key 2003 events;
- securing print, broadcast and online interview/briefing opportunities;
- coordinating legislative-related meetings;
- creating and disseminating e-newsletters to key TAASA stakeholders and information about TAASA member agencies;
- securing participation in Green Ribbon Week (GRW); and
- securing at least one corporate or media partner for TAASA.

Operational strategy

The campaign was unveiled to the public at TAASA's annual conference during a February press conference. A 'PR 101' course for TAASA member agencies was held to educate attendees on bringing the campaign to their communities. Course kits were mailed to agencies, including copies of the PSAs and press kit materials for use locally. An 11-city media tour for TAASA executives to support Sexual Assault Awareness Month (SAAM) in April was scheduled and implemented. Paid TV and radio advertising ran in April and August and a college newspaper print campaign and campus poster campaign were produced for August and September. Media relations assistance was provided to member agencies for April's SAAM and GRW events and PSA placements (outside paid media buy) were secured on state television and radio stations to extend the reach of the campaign on TV and radio. The TAASA website was redesigned to include public awareness campaign materials for visitors accessing the site from advertising and public relations efforts. Survivors' stories and other news hooks were pitched throughout the year to national, local and regional media to promote the campaign, along with coordinated interviews. Legislative outreach was conducted in Washington, DC and Austin in January and April, and contact was maintained with them via phone and through person-to-person meetings throughout the year. An e-newsletter was designed and distributed in March and August of 2003 to keep key publics informed about the public awareness campaign and its success.

Various organizations were contacted for participation in GRW and SAAM and campaign materials were distributed to universities and organizations across the state to increase knowledge of the issue, including speaking engagements at Texas colleges in Autumn/Winter 2003; local-level media outreach was made for these engagements to secure participation and support from local member agencies at college events. Press kits in English and Spanish, press releases, e-newsletters, brochures and other core materials were developed and presentations were given to potential sponsors for the campaign.

Evaluation outcomes

- There was a threefold increase in April and a twofold increase in August for hotline calls over those same months in 2002. Call volume doubled from March to April 2003 and increased almost 30 per cent from July to August 2003.
- TAASA website traffic increased threefold at the ad campaign launch and increased 20 per cent from July to August 2003 during

the second airing of the campaign. Weekly traffic increased 105 per cent from January to April 2003.

- Several rape crisis centres reported that survivors came forward to seek help, citing the public awareness campaign as their reason for speaking out.
- TV advertising was placed in the four largest markets: Dallas, Houston, Austin and San Antonio. Radio advertising was placed in 16 additional Texas markets.
- More than 800 free TV spots and nearly 5,400 radio spots ran.
- Over $1 million in-kind donations helped to extend the life of the campaign.
- Clear Channel Communications became a media partner by donating outdoor advertising, additional online advertising and radio interview time.
- 118 print, 104 broadcast, 2 wire and 99 online placements were secured for the campaign reaching more than 85 million people. Coverage included publications that targeted key audiences, including *ItsTeen.com, BellaOnline.com, Girlzone.com, Go-girl.com, Telemundo, Univision* and *National Hispanic Corporate Council.*
- National media placements included ABC's 'Good Morning America', *Lifetime* magazine, CNN, US News and World Report, and Associated Press.
- Significant print articles on the campaign were placed in major daily Texas newspapers including *Houston Chronicle, Dallas Morning News, San Antonio Express-News* and *Austin American-Statesman.*
- A media tour was conducted in 11 Texas markets to publicize the campaign in April 2003; it secured 12 TV, 34 radio, 23 print and 43 online placements.
- Approximately 30 legislative briefings with ongoing communications with policymakers were secured via e-mail, phone and material mailings.
- More than 3,000 pieces of TAASA literature were distributed to more than 20 Texas colleges and universities to educate students on the issue of sexual assault.
- A statewide tour of over 17 college and university campuses featured survivors sharing their stories with students.
- Media relations assistance to local TAASA agencies for SAAM were provided (11 key markets and 20 rural communities) and GRW events (outreach to 20; secured participation from 7).
- Two e-newsletters were distributed to approximately 400 TAASA contacts including member agencies, board members, media and supporters.

REFLECTION

Based on the information provided:

i.   Do you think that different tools and techniques are required for charity PR vs business PR and if so, by applying Figures 2.5 and 2.8, discuss what they are and why?
ii. Who were the boundary spanners at TAASA?
iii. By focusing on Figures 2.6 and 2.7 and given the sensitivity of the subject matter, what processes helped to increase hotline and website traffic?
iv. Was ordinary or extraordinary management of the PR campaign a contributory factor in its' success?
v.   What intangible assets are likely to add value to TAASA's member agencies and how could they be reported as tangible outcomes?

3

Reputation management: a celebrity-driven society

The public relations profession operates in a celebrity-driven world where even business leaders are groomed for public acceptability and promoted as icons. Public relations practitioners are often confused and bemused by the links between corporate image, corporate identity and reputation, but it is clear that the accumulation of empirical research on corporate image formation has led to the corporate identity literature of today.

The following definitions are adapted from current English usage in *Collins English Dictionary:*

Celebrity   Fame or notoriety.
Image   A mental picture or idea produced from imagination or personality and presented by the public to/of a person, group or organization by others.

Identity   A state of having unique identifying or individual character-istics by which a person or thing recognizes or defines him/her/itself.

Reputation   Notoriety or fame, especially for some specified positive or negative characteristic. Repute is the public estimation of a person or thing to be as specified, usually passive.

CORPORATE IMAGE

Image has had a bad press in public relations terms, yet image consultants continue to be in great demand. There are a number of reasons for this. The technological era has made people everywhere aware of, if not educated about, the roles of government and big business in society. Organizations today have become sensitive to the fact that corporate image operates in different dimensions for different audiences, to arrive as close as possible to what Boorstin (1963) describes as pseudo-ideal, which must be synthetic, believable, passive, vivid and ambiguous. Part of the bad press may lie in the fact that image can be as abstract a concept as Boorstin suggests and therefore lays itself open to suspicion. Bernstein (1991) calls it a vaporous concept of imprecise language, superficial thinking and self-styled image makers who contribute to the insubstantiality. However, Mackiewicz (1993) believes that a strong corporate image is an essential asset in today's era of borderless competition and argues, so what? However nebulous, image is reality because people can only react to what they experience and perceive. Rogers (1993) said, 'I do not react to some abstract reality but to my perception of this reality. It is this perception which for me is reality.'

Thus the nature of corporate image itself, however unpalatable, remains a growth area of public relations productivity which, in combination with a growing body of knowledge about stakeholder expectation and cultural diversity, remains a popular focus of interest. Even companies that prefer to adopt a low profile are assessing their corporate image and its significance when studying their stakeholders' perceptions of their company policies, procedures and behaviour. Other writers find that the low profile most usually associated with such companies evokes words such as 'avoidance', 'uninvolved', 'passive', 'yielding' and 'not influential', and companies may spend as much time and money on maintaining their low profile as they could maintaining a higher one.

Belief systems play a part in people's attitudes. Unfavourable beliefs can lead to a drop in sales or a lowering of share price, which can be corrected by public relations involvement. Many writers and practitioners argue that beliefs make up product and brand images and that people act on those images. The checks and balances in any strategic campaign allow for modification of organizational behaviour or public perception to adjust knowledge, feelings or belief accordingly. Writing during the same period, Eiser suggested that a situation in which there is no communication loop between individuals' expressed attitudes and their behaviour will lead to a situation where stakeholders can only communicate their preferences through actions rather than words.

More current studies show that image does not consist of a single reality held by individuals, but that they hold a series of linked pictures consisting of many elements or objects which merge together and are interpreted through language.

IMAGE AND BRANDING

Corporate image in the professional public relations sense goes back to the 1950s and the introduction of new commercial television stations. Marketing firms jumped on the bandwagon of creating brand image without any systematic theoretical foundation, so that people like Newman (1956) reported that 'the business firm may have no body to be kicked but it does have a character'. Boulding (1956) said, 'the relationship between corporate image and the behaviour of the consumers, saying that what the individual, especially a celebrity on television, believed to be true, was true for him'.

When advertisers picked up the notion of image as a tool for branding products as well as corporate identity, writers of the day like Mayer (1961) saw the brand as a visible status symbol. Thirty years later Gorb (1992) was to argue that the business of corporate image design had become trivialized by too close association with external visual symbolism like logos. He recognized that the dynamics of image lie within the firm itself and have as much to do with manners and interrelationships as with markets. Bernstein's (1991) view is that the image can be built into a product, whereas it can at best only be adjusted for a company, whereas Macrae (1991) believes that a corporate brand can be translated into a mission of pride for staff in the pursuit of excellence, advancing company reputation among stakeholders. From this a branded corporate image can grow into reality.

With the derogatory representation of image as being artificial, the work of O'Sullivan *et al* (1994) was seminal in that it approached the subject of image in terms of its original meaning as being a visual representation of reality, which is important in understanding the world around us, whether employee or shareholder of a company.

An interesting case in point is the British retail conglomerate, Marks & Spencer plc, whose corporate image design had hardly become what

Gorb called 'trivialized' and whose dynamics within the firm had more to do with manners and interrelationships than markets. Nevertheless, it currently has to rework its existing image if it is to evolve and adapt to meet its corporate values while meeting the expectations of its stakeholders, especially its customers who have deserted it.

Mackiewicz's definition of corporate image as 'the perceived sum of the entire organization, its plans and objectives' is very relevant to this case. By arguing that corporate image encompasses the company's products, services, management style, corporate communication and actions around the world, he could be describing any organization in crisis where the positive sum of these perceptual components must be re-evaluated to give the company back the market advantages it once enjoyed or to increase market share and investor popularity. A neutral corporate image can develop over time to become what Boorstin (1963) would describe as so impartial that it repels nobody. Indeed, Kotler (1988) suggests that corporate image can be highly specific or highly diffused and that some organizations may not want or need a very specific image. Some organizations prefer a diffused image so that different groups can project their needs into the organization, and this has clearly taken place in the British people's psyche.

CORPORATE IDENTITY

If there is a clear correlation between business and policy and corporate image in terms of corporate strategy, perhaps the first question the strategist must ask is, 'What business are we now in?' before asking the question, 'What is our identity to ourselves and others?' If an organization is unclear about its identity, then it will not be able to assess its image as perceived by the different stakeholders, nor how these perceptions should be prioritized in terms of strategic planning, policy and practice. For any business strategy to be effective, it must be comprehended accurately by the target publics, or at least in the way that the corporate vision and mission determine.

VISUAL IDENTITY

Whatever type of leader the CEO happens to be, he or she represents the cultural values of the organization and underpins the cultural web that emanates from his or her office. Cultural webs play an important part in understanding corporate identity; a visual identity step model might look something like that shown in Table 3.1.

Table 3.1 *A visual identity step model*

Corporate identity	Objectives	Key issue	Methodology
Situation analysis	Analysing corporate expression and customer impressions	Determining perception of the firms and competitors' aesthetic output	Corporate expressions/ customer impressions research
Designing the aesthetics strategy	Creating distinct impactive aesthetic impressions	Selecting strategically appropriate styles and themes	The styles and themes inventory
Building the collection of design elements	Implementing the strategy with rules of balance	Organizing and managing the implementation	The aesthetics balance sheet
Aesthetics quality control	Monitoring, tracking and adjusting corporate aesthetics over time	Evaluation of prior outputs in the framework and fine-tuning including updating	Aesthetics impact tracking

Corporate visual identity supports reputation through the interrelated dimensions of visibility, distinctiveness, authenticity, transparency and consistency, according to research by van den Bosch, de Jong and Elving (2005). They assert that visual identity supports reputation through 'impressive design, effective application on a range of identity carriers and the condition of these carriers' (p 115).

SEMIOTICS: LOGOS AND LIVERY

The study of signs and symbols, especially the relations between written or spoken signs and their referents in the physical world or the world of ideas, is of increasing importance in the global marketplace. Awareness and respect for cultural similarities, differences and the value people place on logos and livery, is of pressing concern to marketeers and others who aim to influence customers and other stakeholders outside the home country. In a world of information overload, competition between brands at product and corporate level is fierce. In many instances, public relations budgets have had to prioritize rebranding by judicious and creative change in design and colour of logos and livery, both at product (micro) and organizational (macro) levels.

For the 2006 rebranding of Germany 'Land of Ideas – Time to Make Friends' campaign, the Second World War images proved hard to shake off. Public relations research showed that young people no longer carried some of the 60 years old burdens of guilt felt by their parents and grand-parents and loved the 'You are Germany' government advertising promo-tion for the five World Cup matches at Leipzig stadium. It promoted a new Deutschland with modern music, art, film, a woman from the East as Chancellor and a British-style multiculturalism (Channel 4 UK News, 1 April 2006).

In Germany, the research, monitoring and evaluation of image and identity was a complex interactive psychological and behavioural activity. Messages must reach many different stakeholders on many different subjects while retaining a core image, even though those stakeholders' expectations are different. In making what O'Sullivan *et al* (1994) called the 'visual representation of reality', corporate image, based on clear identity, must be made tangible and quantifiable. Only then is it possible to realize competitive advantage.

SUBSTANCE VS STYLE

At the organizational level, Dowling (1993) suggested that in measuring corporate image and culture internally, the effects of mass communication achieved through advertising and corporate identity programmes and changing customer perceptions of the company by employees must be taken into account. If change is desired, rigorous control is essential. If the wrong variables are changed or the sequence of change is wrong, the result can be costly failure. A company's communication strategy tries to cover every aspect of an organization that its stakeholders are or should be aware of. Stanley (1991) argued that no organization can fool its stakeholders with hype. Corporate communication is only effective if it conveys a message of strength and substance based on sound and accepted corporate values and objectives, both internally and externally, based on best practice.

Stuart (1999) believes that corporate identity models, by including variables of organizational culture, corporate strategy, corporate

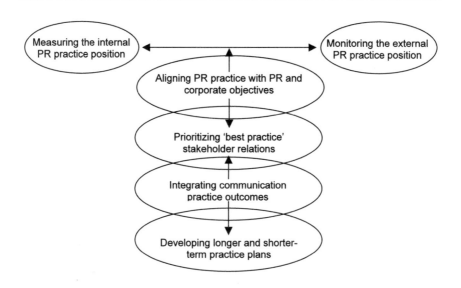

Figure 3.1 *PR operational strategy process*

communication and integrated communication, provide a more definitive model of a modern management process. In the era of global communications these corporate values have come to the fore. The internet has made debates on social responsibility and accountability a new type of challenge for corporate image campaigning. Ethical issues can arise from any part of an organization's business activity and thus form part of the core business operation.

There is hardly one aspect of public relations or corporate communication that can avoid addressing corporate identity, whether in terms of the letter of the law or the spirit of sound corporate citizenship. It is increasingly recognized that the value of ethics statements goes beyond the interest of employee stakeholder groups to embrace all other stakeholders, if not society as a whole, by adding value to an organization. Houlden (1988) recognized that being proactive about the way society views their company is a key skill for modern-day organizational leaders if corporate image is not to be damaged. Singer (1993) calls this 'consequentialism', meaning that ethical judgement goes beyond individual likes and dislikes to produce social mores and norms which form the core of any corporate value system, no matter where or how a company operates.

REPUTATION

Nowhere has the issue of measurement methods in practice been more debated than in the area of US multinational companies and the reputations that they attract. The readers of the journal *Fortune* are asked to rate the largest companies in their own commercial sector on eight key factors using a scale of 0–10 for quality of management; quality of products or services; financial soundness; ability to attract, develop and keep talented people; use of corporate assets; value as long-term investment; innovativeness; community and environmental responsibility.

This particular technique, called the *Fortune* Corporate Reputation Index, along with other measures such as the UK's *Financial Times*/PricewaterhouseCoopers seven-factor model of business performance, have been criticized by Van Riel (1995). Drawing on the criticisms of Maathuis (1993) and Fryxell and Wang (1994), he argues that although these surveys are based on the opinions of so-called experts, 'it is likely that different results would be obtained were the same measurement instrument used by a different group'. Further, 'as a consequence, reputation scores as evaluated by the *Fortune* respondents relate more directly to reputation as a measure of an investment'.

Van Riel fails to make a positive correlation between the concepts of image, identity and reputation in measurable terms and even appears in places to use the words interchangeably. However, his work on applied image research and the various methods in frequent use, warns practitioners that the quality of research is determined not only by the methods used but also by the quality of the questions formulated. The degree of detail in the question determines the degree of possible refinement in the answer, he argues, and states that, 'if a company requires further information about its reputation, then it must embark upon research in greater depth'. A typical approach is demonstrated in Figure 3.2, produced by Echo Research, global specialists in reputation audit and analysis.

This inevitably has implications for the selection of consultants, who in the main are seen to be more objective about assessing the reputation of an organization and therefore more usually given the research task. Ewing, Caruana and Loy (1999) argued that research is more thorough if the consulting firm has no prior connection to the company and is totally unfamiliar to the client. In such instances the client is likely to get more people involved in the selection process. Also, consulting firms with international links are favoured not only by clients who have interests in overseas projects but also by those who actually participate in large domestic projects. 'Firms that have foreign partnerships are preferred over the local ones because they are deemed to have the international expertise to offer clients better services in the long run' they argue. Their study also

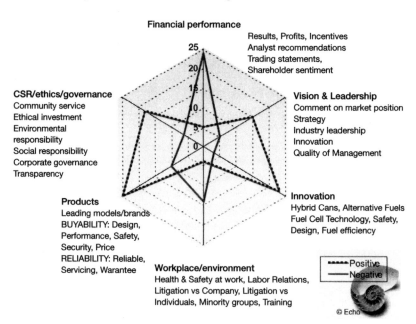

Corporate Reputation Drivers (Automotive Manufacturers) by volume of Positive vs Negative comment

Figure 3.2 *Corporate reputation drivers*

reveals that reputation is not a measure of risk and that 'both factors are separate constructs altogether'.

Ewing *et al* found that if a company does not think or recognize that it has a problem, it will be suspicious of an outsider who tells it that it does have a problem and become more cautious of unsolicited advice. In today's climate of corporate accountability, no organization can afford to take such an arrogant or complacent view of communication nor fail to address its strategic public relations implications.

CAMPAIGN: STANDARD BANK, SOUTH AFRICA

This was a South African story told through a campaign which captured the hearts and minds of staff members and South Africans during the national build-up to the celebration of 10 Years of Democracy. Standard Bank enabled the employment of over 800 South Africans and raised morale for tens of thousands of people. As people rose to the challenge, they set goals and targets amongst themselves through heightened awareness of the client's brand, its sponsorship and corporate social investment practices.

Challenge vs opportunity

As an integral part of South Africa's fabric for the past 141 years and represented in 38 countries, Standard Bank has evolved into a well-known and respected banking brand across the globe. Locally, the brand had been voted the number one financial services brand in the Markinor Brands and Branding Survey for the previous seven years and also featured in the Top 10 Most Admired and Trusted South African Brands rankings.

South Africa's 10th anniversary of freedom fell in 2004, and on 14 April it celebrated its third free and fair democratic election. In anticipation of this, Standard Bank briefed the Magna Carta group of companies to conceptualize and implement a national, holistic media and public relations strategy.

Research

Research information was largely drawn from AMPS and Adex to establish South Africa's major banks' positioning in the marketplace according to share of voice, media usage and activities, and target market demographics, mindsets and insights.

Strategic plan

The key public relations programme objectives were to:

- launch the campaign to media, public and staff;
- build brand equity and entrench the bank's leadership position;
- build awareness via consistent brand messages and encouragement to participate in the promotion;
- effectively amplify existing key events and strategies across the bank's main sponsorships; and
- illustrate examples of what the bank was doing, about which the South African public (and staff) should feel proud and optimistic.

Evaluation

Some of the findings showed that:

- there was a 65 per cent male skew of married men with children but there was no distinct racial skew;
- average household income was R10,672 with a personal income average of R6,662;
- the average age of the primary target market was 30, and 35 in the secondary market;
- 40 per cent took an interest in cricket, 34 per cent in rugby and 40 per cent in soccer;
- 37 per cent had access to the internet, primarily to be informed for e-mail, and were fairly well banked, with 75 per cent having a savings account, 30 per cent having a cheque account, 23 per cent having credit cards and 69 per cent accessing their accounts via an ATM.

The primary campaign message was: 'Standard Bank is South Africa's biggest supporter. We are proud and optimistic about the future of this country and its people, and will continue to invest in the further development and sustainability of South Africa, and this is why'. A secondary campaign message was that supporters should 'Purchase a bracelet and wear it as a symbol of your pride and optimism for the future. The proceeds from the sale of all beaded bracelets will go to Standard Bank for distribution to worthy organizations.'

Operational strategy

The campaign was launched in mid-January and culminated on 27 April 2004, South Africa's Freedom Day. Standard Bank promoted its substantial corporate social investments to demonstrate what the organization had done and continued to do, to make South Africa a better place. It also provided a platform for members of the public and staff from all walks of life to express their personal optimism and pride by helping to make a difference to the future of the country.

An emotive television commercial, ending in the line '44 million people. One nation. One truly committed bank', was created to show that while there were many cultures and traditions living side by side, there was much more than a shared history holding South Africans together than keeping them apart. TV execution was supported by cinema, outdoor, print and radio.

The same theme was carried through the whole of the public relations campaign. Emphasis was placed on showcasing Standard Bank's ongoing sponsorship of sport (predominantly cricket), jazz and the arts, as well as the bank's investments in educational initiatives. A single, innovative medium was chosen to drive home the message – namely blue beaded bracelets designed for individuals to wear as symbols of their pride in South Africa and optimism for its future.

A local independent company was commissioned to hand-make over a million bracelets, creating employment for over 800 previously unemployed and unskilled people in the process. The bracelet contract was the largest order of its kind ever placed in the country. Demonstrating the enormity of the project, the raw material requirements to fulfil the contract were equally large. It took nine days to airfreight the five tons of beads needed from China to South Africa and some 35 kilometres of elastic, weighing in at one ton, were used.

Staff members and the general public were encouraged to purchase bracelets for a minimum donation of only R2 each from a number of sites across the country, including the bank's national branch network, at interactive exhibition stands created for use at the five One Day International cricket matches against the West Indies, at 12 national shopping centres, at selected jazz events, and at the Standard Bank Gallery.

All the proceeds realized through the sale of the bracelets were to be given to the Mathematics Centre for Professional Teachers, a national organization dedicated to developing South Africa's disadvantaged youth. Since 1996, Standard Bank had contributed R679, 500 towards the Maths Centre's educational development grants. It was arranged for groups of 50 underprivileged schoolchildren from rural communities to attend their very first high-profile cricket match as guests of the bank. Chosen from schools selected by the Cricket Legacy Project, the children were treated to a full day of excitement at the five regional one-day international games against the West Indies.

Importantly, ownership of the campaign was driven through an internal drive targeting Standard Bank's 36,000 employees. Information regarding the entire campaign was communicated using the bank's internal satellite television channel, corporate journal, back office posters, banners, etc. Every staff member was encouraged and challenged to purchase bracelets and to promote the concept among customers, clients, friends and family. All staff enjoyed a typical South African Freedom Day celebration party prior to the public holiday.

Evaluation outcomes

The campaign raised positive national and regional media coverage (print, broadcast, electronic public relations) to the value of R500,000+ and raised funds totalling R1,362,340.80. Sharanjeet Shan, Executive Director of the Maths Centre, said:

Literally tens of thousands of children are to benefit from the donation. Less than 2 per cent of black South African students receive a higher grade in mathematics. Without materials, complex abstract concepts cannot be internalized and concretized in the mind. Thanks to Standard Bank and South Africa, much-needed materials and training to schools will be supplied and mathematics learning in our country is set to improve.

REFLECTION

Based on the information provided:

i.   Explain the campaign's links between image and identity in raising the morale of tens of thousands of South African people.
ii. Discuss the differences and similarities between corporate branding and product branding.
iii. In what ways did corporate visual identity support the reputation of the Bank.
iv. What role did semiotics play in the campaign's success?
v.   How did the Bank's campaign operational strategy improve its own business performance while contributing to longer term social investment?

4

Internal communication and PR: employees as ambassadors

The flexibility required of workers, whether management or otherwise, has brought about a resurgence in the recognition of the central role of employee relations based on symmetrical communication for a participative management culture essential to a democratic organization.

MAYHEM VS MORALE

The best 21st century 'learning organizations' value and capture the intellectual and imaginative resources often lying dormant in their workforces. Few HR models move from rhetoric or ideology to the reality of today's competitive workplace without the intervention of expert communicators. Earlier in the book, it was pointed out how necessary it is for an organization to ask itself what business it is in, so as to articulate its mission as a basis for strategic planning.

In-house public relations specialists need to ensure that they have enough authority and influence to ensure that strategic plans and policies work through from the CEO to individuals at all levels of the organization. The public relations director, working alongside the CEO and being fully conversant with the organization's culture and value system, is able to identify any changes required to that system for the mission to be achieved. Having sight of the strategic plan, the public relations team assesses the implications of the plan for public relations structure, process and resources. An appraisal of the tools and techniques required to motivate staff, retain key skills and ensure competency for enhanced productivity, performance and commitment through IT, newsletters, reward, skilfully targeted messages and other techniques, is a normal part of such assessment.

PRIVACY AND CONFIDENTIALITY

The principal strategic HR theories, models, plans and policies are complementary to those of public relations. They often require senior public relations managers to work closely with senior HR managers, especially in areas such as employee relations, collective bargaining disputes and other legal affairs. For example, in Europe the individual has a basic right to control personal information about him or herself under 'rights' based EU legislation, but this does not necessarily resolve conflicts between individuals. The right 'to have' is not the right 'to demand', and individual rights can be overridden by public interest (UK Data Protection Act, 1998, Schedule 2 and 3). Other aspects of this legislation include confidentiality, a duty not to disclose personal information and duties in processing personal data, namely the collection, use and disclosure of personal data.

With the increase in virtual organizations and the imperative to link employees in distant parts of a global organization, the need to control from the centre requires sensitive and expert handling if it is not to corrupt the values upon which most organizations in the West rely. In cultural terms, the corporate communication system becomes part of the core corporate business strategy binding the organization together. Quality of relations between HR and public relations departments in such matters is clearly of strategic and operational significance in the auditing of organizational performance, both internally and externally.

COMMUNICATION AS A CORE COMPETENCY

It is interesting to see how few academic texts on human resource strategy include communication as a key board-level competency. Strategic HR planning, policy making and practice tend to be discussed in relation to recruitment and selection, performance appraisal, assessment compensation, training and development, succession and career profiling, job design and evaluation. These are cited as being essential support activities for operationalizing corporate strategy, but HR frequently fails to identify the contribution of communication for the analytical resources necessary to cope with leadership and the demands of constant change. An experienced public relations practitioner could argue that this is why so many large-scale change programmes fail, including business process re-engineering and total quality management programmes. The role of public relations in helping organizations to change and to sustain new behaviours is nearly always underestimated.

Many key competencies for integrated human resource management strategy parallel key areas in public relations such as:

- specialists from both areas need to share sound leadership through the application of a clear organizational mission;
- competent managing of people, skills, abilities and knowledge through the gathering of intellectual capital;
- monitoring and measuring information to ensure that work groups identify with and 'own' the information best suited to their function and accomplishment of the mission; and
- maintenance of a culture that contributes to an open system in which people feel they are able to say what they feel if it is in the best interests of their responsibilities and can offer potential for growth and development.

Human resources and public relations together oil the wheels of successful change programmes.

COMMUNICATING CHANGE

Large-scale change internal communication programmes must address short-term critical issues which in turn must be faced and understood by all managers. At the same time, global and long-term business communication programmes, published as documents, must demonstrate sensitivity to the needs of individuals. Change programmes must create a realistic view of what can be achieved and not rely too heavily on raising expectations. They must offer opportunity for behavioural learning rather than representational learning; that is, change what people do rather than awareness alone through the use of new words and language. The tension between what people say and what people do is a standard evaluation measure. There has to be devolved accountability of managers at the sharp end to avoid top-heavy and exclusive project teams who drive programmes without consultation and often with inadequate research. Change programmes must be open to changing environmental pressures and priorities and take into account sensitivities that emerge from short-term pragmatists and long-term cynics who refuse to engage emotionally.

A 2006 dispute between London's underground tube train workers and management reflects a former 1994 signal workers' dispute in British Rail. Crossman and McIlwee (1995) identified nine key motivating forces at such times, in which public relations clearly plays an important role. These are:

1. political forces;
2. economic forces;
3. cultural forces;
4. mission and strategy;
5. organization structure;
6. how human resources are managed in terms of flexibility, quality, commitment and strategic integration;
7. stakeholders' interests;
8. community relations;
9. union relations.

Much analysis in the human resource literature about the case fails to incorporate public relations criteria and so rarely offers resolution incorporating joint metrication.

CHANGE DEVELOPMENT PLANS

All internal communication relies on basic principles of public relations, which include clearly defined stakeholders' groups, both formal and informal, plus appropriate channels for information delivery (one-way) and symmetrical communication (two-way). However, given that change is a permanent scenario in many organizations, communication managers need all the public relations skills at their disposal to ensure that staff contribute to decision making, ownership of the outcomes and subsequent supportive action for any change development plan.

This means astute monitoring of structure and process, ongoing training and development, and comparative tracking of stress, absenteeism and turnover. Internal communication is sometimes subjugated, as low priority, to human resources departments to the detriment of the staff and organization as a whole. Employee communication strategy is a specialist area within the overall function of public relations, responsible and accountable to the main board. At critical phases in the change process, the public relations/communication director will need to put together an action plan on the lines of the example shown in Figure 4.1.

FAIRNESS VS FLEXIBILITY

One of the first of eight data protection principles defines 'fairness' as collecting data only when provided. Data subjects should know who controls the data, what data will be collected, who will have access to it, and for what purposes it is being collected. It must be collected lawfully, which means complying with common law duties of confidentiality and complying with the Human Rights Act 1998, in which Article 8 requires the 'right' to respect for private and family life, home and correspondence.

Perhaps the most familiar name to public relations specialists is Atkinson's 1984 'flexible firm' model. This UK model proposed that

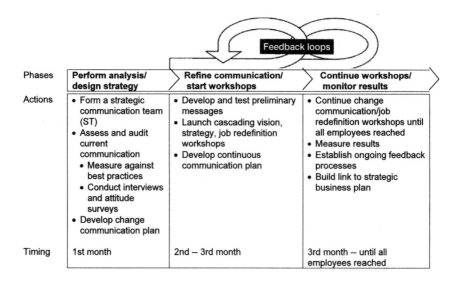

Phases	Perform analysis/ design strategy	Refine communication/ start workshops	Continue workshops/ monitor results

Actions	• Form a strategic communication team (ST)
	• Assess and audit current communication
	  • Measure against best practices
	  • Conduct interviews and attitude surveys
	• Develop change communication plan
		• Develop and test preliminary messages
		• Launch cascading vision, strategy, job redefinition workshops
		• Develop continuous communication plan
			• Continue change communication/job redefinition workshops until all employees reached
			• Measure results
			• Establish ongoing feedback processes
			• Build link to strategic business plan

Timing	1st month	2nd – 3rd month	3rd month – until all employees reached

Figure 4.1 *Three-phase communication change strategy*

Source: Adapted from Barrett (2004) in Oliver (2004)

employers seek an optimal balance between functional, numerical and financial forms of flexibility by segmenting the labour force into core and peripheral groups. The corporate message must be consistent but may have to be transmitted in different ways to these different groups, whether they are performing in-house or as outsourced labour, such as associates or consultants.

Although the concept of permanent change took root fairly readily with writers such as Rosabeth Moss-Kanter, Barry Stein and Todd Jick, the proliferation of models that followed has sometimes assumed that all organizations are being affected by change to the same degree and in the same way because, among other things, of new technology. This is patently not the case, but clearly the larger the organization, the larger the change needed to alter character and performance, given organizational and decision making complexity.

A symbolic approach to decision making sees change as a process of developing myths, metaphors, rituals and ceremonies to cope with the uncertainty and ambiguity that planning and control measures cannot cope with. It is important that the public relations planner is aware of which approach drives decision making in his or her organization if he or she is to articulate appropriately the meanings in the messages being put across. Whichever is the dominant force, communication is the essential leverage and link for any decision making, given that employees and managers will have participated in the decision-making process to ensure the change is 'owned' and can thus be successfully operationalized.

Another key area familiar to public relations consultants will be the concept of 'commitment', based on attitude, behaviour and exchange, as a means of achieving flexibility and change. Exchange theory is seeing revitalized interest because it focuses on concepts of loyalty arising from mutual understanding and benefit. Organizations that demanded total commitment, often at the expense of work-life balance, family and social stability, have come under fire in the recent past and employers are now beginning to realize that there has to be beneficial exchange of one sort or another, material or otherwise, between both parties. Unlike economic exchange, social exchange involves unspecified obligations, the fulfilment of which depends on trust, because it cannot be enforced in the absence of a binding contract. Some organizations have therefore formally introduced the concept of the psychological contract as part of appraisal, whereby transactional contracts are linked to economic exchange but relational obligations or relational contracts are linked to social exchange. The public relations value-added component is measured by techniques which include levels of morale, performance and productivity, as well as traditional communication audits and suggestion schemes, employee rewards and recognition through awards gained by meeting sales targets and other objectives.

The organizational development movement of the 1970s focused on organizational change through the need to integrate systems and groups, including shared problem solving, which demanded higher levels of quality and leadership. The 1990s version of organizational development is about the dynamic links between business decisions, external forces and organizational consequences. It is here, in the concept of change and the lifelong learning organization, that public relations expertise is proving critical and high-profile once more in the 21st century.

Along with HR practitioners, public relations practitioners must promise or offer a way of linking the micro activities of individuals and groups to the macro issue of corporate objectives. So how and where do individual communication performance indicators link to strategic management? There are three principal public relations processes which involve communication expertise and organizational behaviour:

- quality assurance through communication audits;
- expediting core values as manifested by the mission and ethics statements; and
- managing new and more democratic systems of worker control through strong leadership and transparent consultation based on sound communication processes.

COMMUNICATION AS TEAM EFFORT

Strategic internal communication, as part of an overall public relations strategy, is a dynamic operational process linked to the business plan through some or all of the following professional activities. These should be carried out in conjunction with core human resource activities, probably in the following order, and prioritized according to circumstances:

- Establish and target formal and informal internal groups.
- Plan an integrated communication programme.
- Communicate effectively by word and deed through line management.
- Manage strategically around size, geography and international issues at home and overseas.
- Assess the competitive environment.
- Make every employee accountable through understanding of public relations and communication know-how.
- Decide the value and function of all publications.
- Establish fair and just employee communication channels, from induction to retirement or redundancy.

- Organize efficient monitoring and management of noticeboards and electronic messaging.
- Maintain suggestion schemes through a rewarding open-communication culture.
- Incorporate crisis management techniques into headquarters record systems, computer networks and commonsense face-to-face briefings.
- Strengthen corporate identity and reputation by providing internal and external information.
- Clarify the relationship and boundaries between external and internal communication, the dual role and the capacity of those responsible to handle the delicate balance.
- Explain policy rules and regulations and be able to talk to people at all levels.
- Monitor attitude through communication audits.
- Evaluate corporate vision regularly with short-term aims.

It is outside the remit of this book to explain the basic concepts of inter-personal and group communication based on the psychology of perception and exchange of meaning. Suffice to say that internal communication as a core function of corporate strategy is no longer a simple question of efficient bottom-up or top-down communication via line management. It tries to involve as many people as possible in a common purpose. Intranet systems help to make this possible.

A strong and influential communication director, backed by a competent team, is the communication conduit for effectively facilitating symmetrical messaging to a CEO and main board for planning purposes. The director does this by managing barometers, collating and analysing intellectual capital that feeds critically into organizational decision making. Some of the difficulties for managers in attempting coordination and communication between many functional groups, units or departments are that they have their own professional ties to expertise and standards that may or may not parallel the objectives of the corporate mission. In-house public relations practitioners provide a forum for airing barriers to communication and provide the expertise in turning potential functional problems into positive contributions to the communication programme, which is fundamental to an organization's corporate strategy.

CAMPAIGN: EDELMAN PUBLIC RELATIONS WORLDWIDE, USA

In pursuit of increasing its level of quality client service, Edelman set a bold goal to be number one for quality reputation in the communication industry by 2007. With 1,900 employees, hundreds of clients and 39 offices worldwide, the firm faced the challenge of evolving its client service programme across geographical boundaries and cultures. Management turned to staff and they worked together to implement 'RUQ?', a commitment to exceed clients' expectations every day. By late 2003, Harris/Impulse Research reported that Edelman's quality reputation among non-clients in the US had climbed to number three from number nine in 2001, a 10 per cent increase.

Challenge vs opportunity

The year Harris/Impulse Research ranked the firm number nine in quality reputation, the public relations industry was going through a recession with cutbacks at all firms. Edelman made a tough decision when others were watching the bottom line. It dedicated staff and revenue to focus on quality client service. Key to the initiative's success would be Edelman employees, client involvement, and a research/evaluation tool, its 'E^2 Client Satisfaction System'.

Research

Research was conducted to identify the challenges faced and to determine the right approaches:

- A 2001 survey would identify client satisfaction drivers by looking at chemistry, client service, quality of the account team, management and overall quality of work.
- Key drivers to choosing a new agency would focus on quality execution, strategic counsel capabilities, quality of client service, creativity and cost.
- A specialist research firm would provide an historical framework and matrix to study customer focus philosophies and the recognition that quality responsibility is shared by all employees.
- A 2002 Edelman employee survey would aim to uncover challenges to delivering quality client service by making quality everyone's job, communicating a global quality vision to staff, ensuring senior management involvement, improving the training programme, dedicating staff to the programme and involving clients.

- Evaluation of the E^2 quality programme was expected to indicate that regularly scheduled client assessments were not being completed, the interview form wasn't user-friendly, no one was dedicated to monitoring/enhancing quality and findings weren't routinely used to better the firm's operational procedures or in HR appraisals to increase employee competency.
- A test of the firm's quality E^2 assessment form identified fine-tuning, multicultural needs.

Strategic plan

Quality was the firm's number one business goal using the research findings and involving all levels of the firm's employees to develop, evolve and implement its client service programme. Entitled 'RUQ?', the initiative used the alphabet to create high concept symbols for the target audience. Edelman staff were asked to 'exceed their clients' expectations every day'. Staff would be supported by policy and procedures, professional development, and an E^2 client assessment tool, ongoing best practice communications including Q updates, newsletters and a Q website.

The objectives were to increase the relevance and effectiveness of the firm's client service programme, enhance Edelman's quality reputation among clients and non-clients, and be number one in quality reputation in communications by 2007 as judged by industry surveys.

Thus the strategic plan would aim to evolve E^2 (the firm's original client service programme), communicate the mutual benefits of quality client service to employees, involve all levels of employees in the programme's process, and seek client feedback on the firm's performance.

Operational strategy

Phase I: to take E^2 to the next level

- Quality, defined by Edelman quality pledge to clients, was placed on staff's desks.
- The Edelman policy and procedures manual was revised. Principles and policies in each of the firm's core business processes were outlined to ensure effective execution in employees' daily work. Support tools were created to assist staff with policy implementation. Professional development was provided (and mandatory) in client service, people development, financial planning and management, business development and leadership. Job descriptions were updated focusing employees on their responsibilities.

- An online E^2 client satisfaction questionnaire, triggered by the firm's client database, was devised. Closed and open-ended questions related to key client satisfaction drivers. When reviews were returned, the CQO could monitor the information to enhance the firm's processes/systems, help raise the bar on client teams' work, enable client relationship managers to know 24/7/365 how client teams were delivering anywhere in the world, and use the findings in employees' HR performance and appraisals.
- An employee quality recognition programme was created to inspire and demonstrate best practices.
- An intranet Q site was designed to showcase the firm's best practices and create a Q exchange for staff.
- More than 40 account and senior management executives were named Q Champions and dedicated time to deploy, implement and localize RUQ? through communications and meetings.

Phase II: to introduce, implement and monitor RUQ?

- 7 January 2003: Q Day introduced employees to the quality programme/elements. The systematic release of E^2 reviews began. CQO monitoring followed with personal memos sent to each team upon the review's return. Training and the policy and procedure manual were rolled out.
- Q Update memos, teaser campaigns, newsletters, etc regularly educated employees on best practices. Q champions/GMs led monthly/quarterly RUQ? meetings in offices to evaluate local Q progress.
- Cumulative E^2 reports on a global, regional, office-by-office and practice basis were filed with managers. Quality challenges were addressed with special training and successes were praised.
- When E^2 reviews indicated clients wanted more emphasis on research and ROI, the Q 'Measurement at the Center' programme with specific tools and training was created and launched in September 2003.
- The E^2 system was updated to capture more data.
- Employees were recognized with Q Awards, in special Q memos, in HR performance appraisals.

Evaluation outcomes

The firm's client service programme proved relevant and effective. More than 450 E^2 client reviews were returned in 2003/4, an increase of almost 500 per cent compared to 2001/2. Between January 2003 and December 2003, Edelman employees received an 8.16 global Q rating from clients on their E^2 client assessment forms – surpassing the 2003 goal of 7. Between January 2004 and 15 April 2004, the Q rating had risen to 8.27.

RUQ? helped teams serve clients better and boosted team morale. A global tech company was so impressed with the team's improvement, he threw them a party; a multinational health client increased the fee by 25 per cent after working out the challenges he and his team faced; a local retailer, new to public relations, now knows how to assess the team; a consulting firm asked its team to counsel it on vendor assessment.

Reputation among clients and non-clients also improved to the point where, during the recession of 2003, Edelman revenues remained flat, outperforming most other firms. Revenues increased among its top 40 clients by 7 per cent and 93 per cent of these top 40 clients participated in E^2 reviews. Follow-up E^2 reviews with the same clients indicated that in less than a year, teams were increasing their overall Q ratings and improving in areas where clients had challenged them. Edelman was chosen Public Relations Agency of the Year in 2003 by The Holmes Group, which cited the firm's quality programme in announcing the award.

At the time this book went to press the company appeared to be ahead of schedule. The 2003 Harris/Impulse survey rated the firm number 3 out of 40 major US public relations firms in quality reputation among non-clients compared with number 9 in 2001. Thus, as judged by industry, Edelman looks to be on target to achieve number 1 for quality reputation in the communication industry by 2007.

REFLECTION

Based on the information provided:

i.   Could Edelman be described as a learning organization and if so why?
ii. How does the theoretical three-phase change strategy described in the chapter, compare with the approach taken by Edelman?
iii. Should communication with employees be the responsibility of an in-house human resource department, a public relations department or outsourced to a consultancy firm?
iv. What evidence is there that the campaign applied teamwork as a best practice concept?
v.   Does the evaluation indicate that short term behavioural learning, as distinct from representational learning, has taken place in support of long term employee performance?

5

Beyond 'customer is king': sales and marketing promotion

Relations between the marketing and public relations industries have had a chequered history in the past 20 years. Some would argue that they have been involved in a power struggle for longer than that.

In 1978, Kotler and Mindak wrote that there were four levels of public relations activity for marketing purposes, the first being for small, often charitable, organizations which, until recently, rarely outsourced professional public relations or marketing services. A second group, mainly from the public sector, do engage public relations services, while a third, small manufacturing companies, often use external marketing services or in-house sales personnel. Fourth, in large *Fortune* 500 companies, public relations and marketing are usually separate departments, which may complement each other. In the past, they were coordinated by the chief public relations officer who would report to the CEO and the main board. Today's integrated communication strategies combine the managerial tactics of market research, advertising and public relations theory and practice, with coordination driven by a dominant coalition.

CONCEPTUAL AUTHENTICITY

A current area of conflict which is emerging from empirical literature, case studies and the growing body of public relations knowledge as an academic discipline is that of the nature of public relations itself. No reputable profession can afford dissonance around its own identity or its public image, so next-generation public relations leaders and opinion formers must commit to a definitive acceptance of the facts of the 'nature' of the public relations industry as distinct from generally accepted notions about its 'nurture'.

There is a popular misconception that, just because approximately two-thirds of public relations agency fee income is used to sell product and only around one-third is going on government, investor/financial, corporate/reputation promotional campaigns, public relations is a simple communication support tool, albeit by a variety of tactical means, to bottom-line sales and turnover in the short term. Most large corporations and institutions now label their traditional public relations departments as 'corporate communication departments' to emphasize the reality that any public relations campaign, whether the spend is on, say, corporate or product branding, must be aligned to the strategic business plan in terms of both time and motion and be overseen by them.

In practice, many generic public relations operational tools and techniques support integrated marketing public relations activity. However, in theory, the body of knowledge required to forward plan and manage a public relations strategy is so aligned to corporate or organizational strategy that the reputation of the whole organization is more than the sum of its parts and certainly of any single product or service. This is not mere semantics nor bureaucratic management speak. The history of public relations is littered with examples of the dangers of losing sight of core organizational goals or corporate objectives due to overzealous, creative marketing, especially during the 1980s/90s. That is not to say that profits from a single product promotion cannot sometimes bring about a healthy injection of much needed capital and income, eg iPod in 2004, but it does not, or should not throw the whole business strategy off course. Profits from one area of a business may be required to go into supporting other areas such as health and safety, technological and environmental developments in other activities, products and services at any given time. Better that the sales and marketing industry referred to 'marketing publicity' or 'market promotion' and dropped the term 'public relations' in its strategic planning and policy making.

The word 'relations' in the term 'public relations' can be used in a shallow or deeply meaningful way, and so the generic term 'public relations' should not be structured as a subsidiary component of a marketing function or applied loosely to the selling of material goods and services. This is not to take the ethical dimension to its furthest, ideological position whereby two-way, symmetrical communication is regarded as the democratic norm in the building of relations based on trust. In any organization, there are threatening or competitive situations in which asymmetrical communication is necessary because of received intelligence. However, as Alvin Toffler wrote some 35 years ago in his seminal work *Future Shock*, 'our first and most pressing need... a strategy for capturing control of change... diagnosis precedes cure' (p 430). He continued, 'we need a strong, new strategy... we can invent a form of planning more humane, more far-sighted and more democratic than any so far in use. In short, we can transcend technocracy' (p 400). There is a message here for marketing public relations professionals, as the following words suggest.

Today's wonderfully creative public relations campaigns that often capture society's hearts and minds must be underpinned by skilful diagnosis based on quality research so as not to intensify 'the rise of a potentially deadly mass irrationalism' (Toffler, 1970, p 430). Whether through traditional methods such as advertising and events management or postmodern methods involving new media and mobile telephones, Toffler's strategy for survival is ever more pertinent in our globalized economy. Unlike legal and social issues, commodities have shorter and shorter product lifecycles in what Toffler called 'our high transience society' (p 67) and reminds us that 'in almost no major consumer goods category... is there a brand on top today which held that position ten years ago' (Schachte in Toffler, p 64) and 'in the volatile, pharmaceutical and electronic fields, the period is often as short as six months' (Theobold in Toffler, p 65).

Organizations are social institutions, whether operating for profit or not-for-profit and, as such, still today it can be argued, depend on:

> continuity, order and regularity in the environment. It is premised on some correlations between the pace and complexity of change and man's decisional capacities. By blindly stepping up the rate of change, the level of novelty and the extent of choice, we are thoughtlessly tampering with these environmental preconditions of rationality. (Toffler, 1970, p 326)

KNOWLEDGE AND SKILL

In the 1990s, a more substantive approach to developmental education and training emerged through the Chartered Institute of Public Relations, for public relations professionals, the Institute of Advertising, for advertising professionals, and the Chartered Institute of Marketing, for marketing professionals.

In blue-chip companies, marketing, advertising and public relations functions are linked autonomously to the corporate and business plans but managed overall as corporate communication. Clearly each function is accountable for its own strategic analysis, segmentation and targeting of those stakeholders for whom it is accountable, but the overall organization's image or reputation must not be compromised by any one function. Of course, all three areas overlap at the boundary between themselves and at the interface between the organization and its environment, with consequences for environmental monitoring and research. It is here that the focus of each function must be independent of the other to maintain plurality of views and richness of information. However, the various perspectives must be brought together at a later stage for integration, then linked strategically with other functions such as HR, since environmental intelligence will have relevance for a range of internal functions.

Strategic planning for all functional areas incorporates analysis, monitoring of individual programme development, implementation control and evaluation. If there is a lack of control over any one area, say one attempting to dominate another for competitive budgeting or status purposes, then the communication strategy is put at risk. A climate of rivalry can be managed as a force for good or ill, depending on whether the culture is based on a closed or open management system.

As the amount of information flowing in and out of every organization increases, far exceeding any public relations strategist's requirements, the key task of any adequate intelligence system is to access and capture only relevant data and direct it to the required location for analysis by the right group at the right time. A focus on capturing and using pertinent marketing communication data, for example, will not necessarily help service the needs of the advertising or public relations group as it may be too customer-specific at the expense of other stakeholders if not moderated by the communication strategist or overseer. Large firms have comprehensive management information systems, and the development of new technologies is increasingly making the selection and identification of critical data easier. Because of the need for longer-term relationships with customers, marketing professionals have been quick to realize the need for systematic design, collection, analysis and reporting of data. Findings relevant to the mutual understanding and sustaining of goodwill, traditionally seen as a customer relations activity, are increasingly coming under the auspices of public relations and referred to by marketers as 'relationship marketing'. This is especially the case in the retail industry, which promotes products and services through loyalty card schemes.

In terms of environmental scanning, market researchers analyse and categorize the economic environment in a number of ways. A common approach to strategic marketing is one where the philosophy implies that all organizations exist because they are offering some form of 'product' to someone else, whether it be direct, such as fast-moving consumer goods, a service offered through a third party and perhaps paid for by a third party (say, government), or a service in the community or to achieve a social objective.

Some of the rivalry referred to earlier between marketing and public relations departments in organizations has been about whether or not the principal stakeholder group or customer 'audience' ought to define the department's name. Traditionally, even though the communication tools and techniques available may be drawn on by all three functions of marketing, advertising and public relations, the dominant strategic force remains with public relations. The public relations function views its constituencies as consisting of a broader range of stakeholder groups or publics than customers, to include competitors and suppliers, employers/ employees, community and local government, central government, financiers, investors and the media. Usually, only qualified public relations graduates are trained to appraise all ongoing stakeholder relations to ensure that the organization's strategic communication plan is coherent and consistent in relation to the strategic business plan. However, increasingly, models such as the integrated marketing communication (IMC) mix model are emerging from marketing academics; see Figure 5.1.

VALUE-ADDED AND IMC

Of particular value to market research professionals has been the public relations evaluation concept of value-added, so the notion of integrated marketing communication (IMC) has established itself as a critical learning and teaching topic. Value-added is an accounting process which involves horizontal analysis of the industry a firm is in, along with a vertical study of the overall distribution chains to see where value can be improved and competitive advantage gained by strategic repositioning or sales reconfiguration.

Another important technique which overlaps with public relations is market segmentation. Guiltinan and Paul (1994) define market segmentation as 'the process of identifying groups of customers with highly similar buying needs and motives within the relevant market'. Segments are formed by identifying response differences between segments. They can be clearly described and reached, and are worthwhile as benefits to the organization. They are stable over time, so marketing programmes can fix costs to be acceptable. They will be classified using descriptive categories based on management's knowledge and experience of customer needs or desires supported by available information (customer group identification), or by the way customers respond. Groups can be identified by working

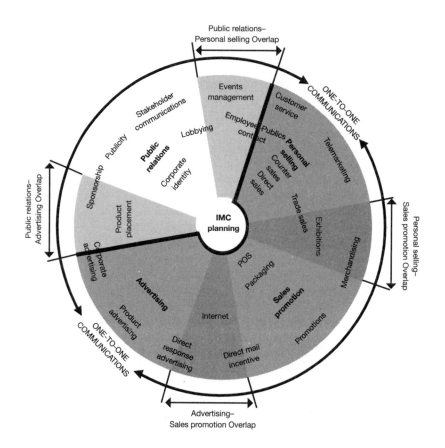

Figure 5.1 *An integrated marketing communication (IMC) mix model*

Source: Pickton and Broderick (2005)

backwards, for example noting characteristics such as the frequency of individual or group purchases or perceptions of brand preference.

Communication theory is grounded in models of perception from clinical psychology, a key factor in public relations academic modelling. Thus, another tool that is increasingly popular is the use of perceptual mapping, where consumer perceptions of product attributes can be analysed psychologically. On the two-dimensional perceptual map, consumers' reception is grouped together with competitive brands to demonstrate position and relationship.

COMPETITIVE ADVANTAGE

Perhaps the most popular competitive advantage theory of the past 15 years has been Porter's (1985) five competitive forces in determining industry profitability, which can clearly be adapted to organizational-level monitoring and evaluation through perceptual mapping and intelligence communication. Perceptual mapping is a technique which identifies gaps in the market to see if there is scope for a new product ,or to plan branding or competing products in terms of particular characteristics such as price and quality. It is a useful concept for integrating marketing communication with corporate communication to ensure that publicity is coherent and consistent with the aims of corporate communication programmes, or 'on message' as the politicians say. Such analysis can produce public relations intelligence that feeds into the research, monitoring and evaluation information paradigm, as shown in Figure 5.2.

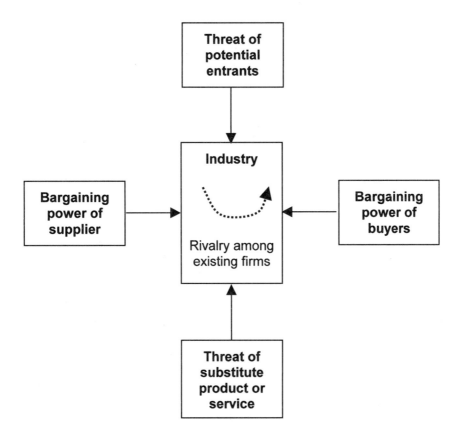

Figure 5.2 *Market intelligence*

The importance of theoretical models such as Porter's lies in its focus on the competitor stakeholder group and the subgroups within it, such as rivalry between existing competitors, the threat of entry from new niche competitors, and the financial muscle of buyers and suppliers. The dynamic nature of competition and thus short and longer-term relationship building is central to both marketing and public relations involvement, including lobbyists acting on behalf of both professions.

Increasingly, interest has been shown by the public relations industry in the notion that marketing tools and techniques can be applied to the competitive internal communication environment of an organization, because of the political nature of competition for jobs and status, thus creating a 'market' of the human resource requiring public relations.

Where once this was the domain of the public relations department, today it is sometimes thought that the marketing department is as likely to be aware of the corporate climate, structure and culture as other experts. Their knowledge and sensitivity to culture, orientation, power and influence will have been accrued from their analysis of customers, organizational structure linked to the marketing plan, and the interfunctional dynamics needed to operate that marketing plan.

Porter's theories of competitive advantage suggest that it is essential that organizations understand how the physical, human, financial and intangible aspects of an organization, including plant, equipment, people and finance, must be appraised together so as to quantify added value to the customer and thus to the organization as a whole.

The focus on data collection tends to be organized around customer databases, which provide insight into customers' behaviour and motivation in many markets, but particularly retail markets with data collated from loyalty card schemes in the grocery sector. One supermarket chain uses the Target Group Index, a research service which matches customer databases to three years of customers' buying behaviour.

With the growth in service marketing and the development of relationship marketing, more and more organizations are adopting customer awareness programmes to harness the organization's effort to deliver improved value to their customers. This coincided with a general global economic recession which meant that, although traditional public relations departments had been removed or downsized, the need for public relations techniques remained. Market research departments found themselves on a fast learning curve to adopt the public relations skills and techniques required to cope with their sales and marketing strategies, given the rapid rise of consumer awareness and pressure groups. Customers not only had access to IT and media, but were now well organized and increasingly vociferous in their demands for value for money. If a particular product or brand attracted bad publicity, this could impact on corporate image,

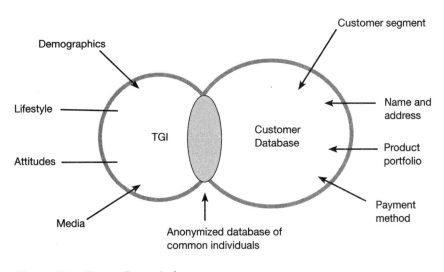

Figure 5.3 *Target Group Index*

Source: Clive Humby BMRB/Dunn Humby Data Analysis Company, UK

identity or reputation to the extent that the overall public relations strategy could be undermined, not least in respect of shareholder investment.

From the point of view of the overall planning process, stakeholder communication must be integrated around core corporate values, objectified by the production of mission statements. Representing the vision of what the organization is or hopes to become, the PRO collates the communication aims and objectives of each function, assesses compatibility and integrates it with the corporate business plan.

CUSTOMER RELATIONS

Porter's model suggests that there are three fundamental ways in which firms achieve sustainable competitive advantage through customer relations. These are cost leadership strategy, differentiation strategy and focus strategy. The difference between strategic marketing which seeks to interpret the organization's generic strategies into market-based strategies based on perceived added value is that it is dominated by price.

Other writers such as Grunig and Repper (Grunig, 1992, Ch 6) believe that the interdependence of stakeholder groups in the achievement of organizational objectives reaffirms the strategic role of public relations in the goals encapsulated by a mission statement.

Most sales and marketing becomes strategic at some point because of the range of options available and so the academic literature concentrates on issues of strategic choice, target market strategy, marketing strategies with demand, positioning strategies and marketing strategies for different environments. The strategy adopted will depend on whether the organization is a market leader with 45 per cent market share, a market challenger with 30 per cent market share, a market follower with 20 per cent market share or a market niche with 10 per cent of the market share (Kotler, 1994). Intelligence data from each market share will drive any public relations imperative.

Other areas of promotional overlap with public relations are in the sales and marketing of fast-moving consumer goods, as previously mentioned, and business-to-business markets. Consumer markets are characterized by heavy advertising and promotion programmes targeted at key segments so as to build brands and speed up the process of innovation and new product development. They also seek strategic relationships and alternative channels of distribution such as direct marketing and selling via the internet.

BUSINESS-TO-BUSINESS RELATIONS

In business-to-business or industrial markets, relationship marketing is critical to success, with particular emphasis on conferences and trade shows. Kotler also identified three types of strategic marketing in service industries by naming the company, employees and customers as being linked by internal marketing, external marketing and interactive marketing. With services marketing, the different attributes of the service are identified or organized to target customer value and to position the organization to obtain differential or competitive advantage.

A public relations service must be able to articulate and prioritize any or all attributes offered by the service or organization in order to target customer value and to position the organization for competitive customer advantage. As organizations increasingly enter global markets, strategic sales and market decisions are based on international research and may include looking for similarities between segments in different countries with a combination of factor and cluster analysis to identify meaningful cross-national segments.

WEB ANALYSIS AND EVALUATION

This has driven the public relations industry to look for new ways of measuring the impact of messages across diverse cultures and in shorter time frames. With export marketing, for example, products are usually sold from the domestic base. With international marketing, products and services are marketed across national borders and within foreign countries. With global marketing, coordination of the market strategy in multiple markets operates in the face of global competition. One of the principal strategic concerns in the latter case is the task of developing the global portfolio, which incorporates a very high level of involvement from sales and marketing and public relations departments in developing e-commerce and evaluating purchasing and promotional web pages as part of the strategic plan.

Eye-tracking, analysing the eye movements and point of gaze of subjects in a market research or public relations study, is now an accepted component in most studies which involve visual presentations. The technology has advanced to the point where data can be analysed in real time for computer or TV-generated images or rapidly analysed with video analysis tools when the subjects have viewed a live scene such as a shopping experience. In Figures 5.4 and 5.5, an evaluation of a *Financial Times* page shows where subjects looked and for how long.

Communication students generally understand the fundamental concepts of e-commerce technical infrastructure and applications. This includes electronic commerce and law, security and authentication, and internet protocols for knowledge-economy companies. These are key competencies for consultant practitioners who are expected to offer strategic corporate e-learning communication solutions for business and commerce. Furthermore, an understanding of the value/supply chain, with all its communication interfaces and the implications of an e-enabled supply chain, is essential to the marketing public relations practitioner. How people receive, interpret and respond to visual information now forms a critical component in market research and relationship evaluation.

EFFICIENCY VS EFFECTIVENESS

The effectiveness of any strategy depends in part on the quality of the monitoring and environment scanning within different environments, which are in a constant state of change. Of particular concern to the public relations practitioner is the problem of control. Not all marketing departments make clear strategy statements that are comprehensive or articulate the interdependence and interaction of the various elements

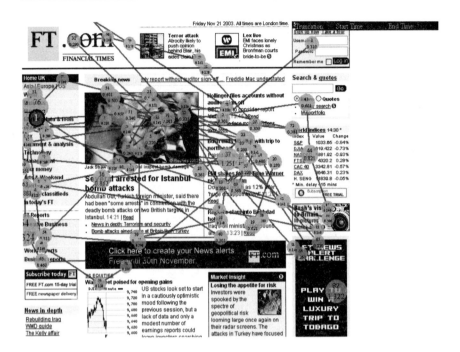

Figure 5.4 *A two-dimensional view of a web analysis page*

Key
Top left No 1 is the mouse click. The other numbers are the sequential numbering
of fixations and duration while the lines between fixations represent the subject's
scan paths

so that the total mix is achieved in a harmonious way. Many a product
promotion has created communication and public relations disasters when
scandals became focused solely on customers and omitted to consider the
knock-on effect of corporate image on other stakeholders.

Development of branding theory and public relations input into practice
have reduced some of this difficulty, but at the same time have created
semantic confusion when describing activities relating to both marketing
and public relations. For example, Cravens (1994) says that, 'a product is
anything that is potentially valued by a target market for the benefits or
satisfactions it provides, including objects, services, organization, places,
people and ideas'. This description covers both tangible and intangible
services and could conceivably include other identifiable stakeholders,
beyond suppliers and customers.

Figure 5.5   *A three-dimensional view of the same web analysis page*

Key
These are 'look zones', showing defined areas selected in the page and the percentage of time spent looking at them. The number 44 indicates time in seconds, while 42 per cent represents the percentage of time relative to the selected areas.

TOOLS AND TECHNIQUES

Brand promotion, including corporate advertising, is a traditional public relations tool for adding value to a product so as to differentiate it from its competitors or to add value to the corporate identity. However, not all marketers see it this way, nor indeed do all other professional departments in the organization. Finance, for example, may be involved in designing pricing strategy, given, as Kotler (1994) says, that 'price is the only element in the marketing mix that produces revenue. The other elements produce costs'.

As with any policy making, planning and strategic development, evaluation and control are of paramount importance. A strategic review of marketing plans is usually conducted every two or three years to provide groundwork for long-term strategy development as well as interim analysis. It will usually consist of a full audit of the marketing environment and operations relating to all aspects of the corporate mission, objectives and strategies, as well as a review of the marketing objectives, strategies, programmes, implementation and management issues.

The role of advertising and publicity is to be cost-effective in creating awareness in the early stages of the product lifecycle, whereas sales promotion is used in the ordering and reordering stages of buyer readiness where the product is mature or in decline. Some of Kotler's views of the tools and characteristics of communication are shown in Table 5.1.

Christopher, Payne and Ballantyne (1994) suggest that 'relationship marketing has as its concern the dual focus of getting and keeping customers'. Indeed, they go on to develop a model which suggests that there are five other markets that impact on the customer market: referral, internal, supplier, employee recruitment, and influence markets, and if marketing people are to tinker with all these particular audiences, the role of the strategic specialist becomes imperative. It is apparent that marketing models are linking segmentation to discrete variables within

Table 5.1   *Tool characteristics*

Tools	Characteristics
Advertising	Public presentation, pervasive, amplified expressiveness. TV, radio, press, cinema, magazines, print, packaging, posters
Product/service publicity	Gain attention, provide information, inducement that gives value, invitation to engage in immediate action; competitions, premiums, gifts, trade shows, coupons, stamps
Direct marketing	Direct at consumer, customized, up to date; catalogues, mailings, telemarkets, electronic shopping
Press and media	High credibility, messages as news not advertising; press kits, seminars, annual reports, sponsorships, lobbying
Customer relations (sales)	Personal confrontation, cultivates relationships, encourages response; presentations, incentives, samples, trade shows
Marketing PR	Product pre-launch by preparing the marketplace for introduction of a new product

Source: Adapted from Kotler (1994)

Table 5.2 *Towards integration*

Bottom-line approach Transaction marketing	Value-added approach Relationship marketing
Focus on single sale	Focus on customer retention
Orientation on product features	Orientation on product benefits
Short timescale	Long timescale
Little emphasis on customer service	High customer service emphasis
Limited customer commitment	High customer commitment
Moderate customer contact	High customer contact
Quality concern of production	Quality concern of all

Source: Christopher, Payne and Ballantyne (1994)

the stakeholder model. Meanwhile, customer communication relies on the traditional bottom-line approach (marketing) versus the value-added approach (public relations), as shown in Table 5.2.

PROMOTION PERFORMANCE

As with public relations and advertising campaigns, reviews are essential in examining the extent to which sales programmes are appropriately directed and whether or not a particular programme has been properly integrated within the organization as a whole. This may include a product promotion review where benchmarking takes place against external examples of best practice, which also involve ethical and social responsibility criteria. Some of the performance criteria and measures used by marketing functions are sales analysis, market share analysis, sales to expense ratios, financial analysis and profitability analysis. This is a costly process, and the results will be compared with various internal budgets, targets and performance measures set by the corporation.

PERFORMANCE GAPS

It is at this point that any positive or negative performance gaps, new opportunities or threats may require corrective action to bring the annual plan or longer-term strategy back in line with objectives. The requirement is often to identify the difference between problems, symptoms and causes that cannot be ignored from seasonal or short-term variations. Third-party intervention from public relations consultants is often bought in, in conjunction with other management consultants.

Where, for instance, some inter-functional relationship problems experienced by marketing and manufacturing departments cannot be managed effectively, consultants can provide an objective solution. Typically, problems that emerge are that products are developed around technological capability, not market needs; products may fail commercially; products may be technically superior but priced too high; and concentration on tangible attributes may supersede the customer benefits. Indeed, some organizations have placed research and development and marketing under one authority, in physical close proximity, or set up coordination teams or task groups on particular projects. The role of public relations may be to advise on internal or external communication processes, including impacts on corporate identity.

MARKETING VS MANUFACTURING

Other areas of inter-functional conflict may arise from:

- marketing who want more capacity, versus manufacturing who want accurate sales forecasts;
- marketing who want faster response, versus manufacturing who want consistent production;
- marketing who want sufficient stocks, versus manufacturing who want cost control;
- marketing who want quality assurance, whereas manufacturing have products which are difficult to make;
- marketing who want variety, whereas manufacturing want economical runs;
- marketing who want low prices and high service, whereas manufacturing often have high costs with extra services; and
- marketing always looking for new products, whereas manufacturing see extra design and tooling costs.

Competent communication skills between departmental heads are crucial, although few will realize that they are involved in public relations.

So what we have seen at a strategic level is the need for integration of all elements of the communication mix while, at a tactical level, some of the tools employed when implementing and evaluating programmes are now shared with public relations experts. As Smith and O'Neill (1997) said:

Marketing used to be simple. So simple, it could even be left to marketing managers, but it isn't like that any more. The business of marketing, namely creating value by managing customer relationships, must be central to corporate management and financial planning. Marketing must be seamlessly woven into every function of those companies intent on getting to the future first.

CAMPAIGN: 3M, USA

3M rolled out a comprehensive promotion programme to strengthen its Scotch® brand and reinforce its positioning as the trusted resource for gift-wrapping. For the previous six years, the Scotch® Brand Most Gifted Wrapper™ Contest had been the centrepiece of the Scotch brand tapes programme. In 2003, in the United States, the contest served as a springboard to launch new tactics to continue building brand equity. Due to the success of the Contest in the United States, it was also run in the UK that year for the first time.

Challenge vs opportunity

In the United States in 1997, 3M launched Scotch pop-up tape, a wristband tape dispenser with pre-cut tape strips, with the goal of positioning it as *the* tape of choice during the holiday gift-wrapping season. 3M and its agency, Hunter Public Relations (HPR) created the Scotch Brand Most Gifted Wrapper Contest, a national holiday kick-off event held in New York City. Since the Contest proved to be a success not only for introducing the new tape dispenser, but also for building equity for Scotch tapes, 3M and HPR continued to stage the Contest for the next six years. In 2003, 3M and HPR concluded that the Contest could serve as a springboard to launch new tactics to continue building brand equity during the holiday season. To gain needed insight into which proposed tactics would deliver best in strengthening the equity of the brand, 3M and HPR conducted extensive primary research, as described below.

Research

The agency hired an independent research firm to conduct an online survey of Americans' perceptions of holiday gift-wrapping and their gift-wrapping habits. Key survey findings helped create new tactics and strategies for the 2003 programme.

They found that 70 per cent of Americans would consider calling a telephone hotline for help with their gift-wrapping needs; one-third of Americans wait until the last two days before the gift-giving occasion to wrap their gifts; and more than 50 per cent of Americans do their holiday shopping after Thanksgiving. Additional research was conducted through an online poll on the Scotch tapes website. Americans were asked to select from a list of five odd-shaped items which they would like to see this year's 'most gifted wrappers' wrap at the Scotch Contest. The two items with the most votes were used in the contest.

Strategic planning

Strategies and tactics were presented to 3M management in early 2003. After receiving 3M's approval, the agency began implementing the proposed tactics with audience and messages in mind, based on objectives to:

- generate high-profile media coverage for Scotch tapes during Q4, which is the key sales and usage period;
- generate national and local media coverage for Scotch tapes during Q4 in the top 25 media markets;
- position Scotch tapes as *the* gift-wrapping expert among consumers; and
- leverage the Contest as a springboard for a series of new holiday-related tactics.

Female consumers aged 25 to 54 years were targeted to use Scotch tapes for all their gift-wrapping needs. The messages would say that the Scotch brand was a trusted resource for those looking to wrap their gifts with flair, speed and style, and could help with gift-wrapping challenges if customers called a Scotch Brand Gift-Wrapping Tips Hotline at 1-866-HOW-2-WRAP.

Operational strategy

The Scotch Brand Most Gifted Wrapper Contest

- Contestants were recruited by distributing a 'Call for Entries' press release to newspapers, asking entrants to describe why they are 'America's Most Gifted Wrapper'.
- The seventh annual Contest was held in the Rockefeller Center, and $10,000 was awarded to the winner.
- With the Contest in its seventh year, the agency needed to find new and interesting pitch angles. To sustain media interest, they

introduced new 'wrinkles' to the contest whereby an online poll provided a new media angle and drove consumers to explore additional aspects of the website. Interesting human-interest stories from finalists were used to pitch as story angles to the media, eg Sue Collins wrapped gifts for Hollywood stars. 'Most Gifted Wrapper' finalists wrapped a 10-gallon hat, skis with poles (selected by participants from the online poll) and a La-Z-Boy® chair to provide the media with interesting visuals.

● The first ever toll-free gift-wrapping hotline would be staffed by previous contestants.

● An audio news release and a press/wire release announcing the availability of the hotline in mid-December would be distributed.

With both the Contest and the hotline taking place during the month of December, timing was a key issue. The agency waited to pitch the hotline until after the contest to try to garner two separate placements from one publication or broadcast station. However, since the hotline was thought to primarily be a print story, ways were sought to expand upon potential media coverage. Adjustments were made during implementation, due to the success of coverage of the hotline in the print media. By developing B-roll footage to distribute to TV stations on 22 and 23 December for a last-minute holiday story, the reach of the hotline benefited from late expansion. Past contest winners would be contracted to serve as spokespersons for Scotch tapes and their unique talents would be utilized to pitch a multitude of creative gift-wrapping angles to the media.

Evaluation outcomes

Media coverage of the Scotch tapes public relations programme was measured through monitoring services and showed that, in 2003, Scotch tapes publicity generated 3,553 placements and 125,926,696 impressions from Q4/holiday media tactics. In the seven-year history of the Scotch tapes public relations programme, this was the largest number of placements and impressions generated from Q4/holiday media outreach.

The 2003 Scotch tapes promotion garnered high-profile media coverage in all top 25 US markets. National television media highlights included CNN Daybreak, The Wayne Brady Show, FOX & Friends Saturday, A&E Biography and Living It Up! With Ali & Jack. High-profile print media highlights included *Newsweek, Time Out New York, Real Simple, Country Woman, USA Today, Atlanta Journal-Constitution, The Minneapolis Star Tribune* and *The Baltimore Sun.* International media highlights included Nippon TV in Tokyo, CNN International, *The Hurriyet & Milliyet* (Turkish newspaper), and RTVI (Russian television). UK contest media highlights included ITV (2x), Love2Shop, Channel 4, Richard & Judy, Des & Mel, BBC Good Homes, *Western Daily Mail, Daily Record* and *Sunday Post.*

REFLECTION

Based on the information provided:

i.   Using the IMC model, identify which tactics have been applied in the Scotch brand promotion contest.
ii. How might the target group index inform customer behaviour for future years?
iii. What tangible significance would statistical website analysis have for the company?
iv. How could brand promotion be sustained so as to add to brand equity to the tapes programme over time?
v.   How might the annual marketing event be developed through strategic public relations to offer competitive advantage the rest of the year?

6

Media relations: a borderless world view

Mass communication media have come to play a dominant role in the life of everyone, including the public relations practitioner. With the growth and convergence of global telecommunications and information technology, the role of these media can only become even more important in the future. Few people, let alone organizations, dare to forecast where this will lead in years to come other than to suggest that the media will play a vital role in the survival of every organization.

Most large organizations employ agencies to monitor the media and to communicate with journalists, proprietors and other significant people in institutions who could be instrumental in the maintenance of an organization's corporate aims and objectives. Strategically, this role can be seen as a defensive, asymmetrical relationship or, in more enlightened far-seeing organizations, as a creative, symmetrical relationship, through which the organization can obtain the information necessary to be able to adapt to a changing environment.

MASS COMMUNICATION

The significance of mass communication media on an organization cannot be overestimated. McQuail (1994) ascribes five characteristics to the media which explain their importance to society as a whole, relevant to the modern organization at all stages of a public relations campaign or programme:

1. *A power resource* – this is highly relevant to organizations, given that the media are the primary means of transmission and source of information in society. A disgruntled shareholder wishing to unseat a member of the board will find it difficult to communicate with other shareholders in the face of the power that the organization's managers can rally.
2. *As an arena of public affairs* – for business organizations, this may seem less important than for governmental organizations which are often the target of media attention, but many recent inter-company controversies involving government agencies have been played out in the arena of the media.
3. *As definitions of social reality* – at first sight, this is a nebulous concept and yet McQuail explains that the media is a place where the changing culture and the values of society and groups are constructed, stored and visibly expressed. What society perceives to be the reality of organizations will be formed from a limited or non-existent personal impression gained from direct contact with the organization and from those images and impressions which the media choose to present. Different sections of the media attempt to project different realities. For example, in the UK, the BBC 'Money Programme' presents a world in which it is normal for companies to compete with each other for profit without implying any criticism of the underlying capitalist principles involved. Left-wing publications will, on the other hand, portray a different version of reality, one that is much more critical and sceptical about the motives and social value of the leaders of major firms.
4. *As a primary key to fame and celebrity status* – this used not to be particularly important for business organizations. However, increasingly, leaders of organizations have used the media to project a desirable image. This is also true for authors of strategic management theory texts who have become highly rewarded 'gurus' on the international lecture circuit.
5. *As a benchmark for what is normal* – this is particularly important for organizations where ethical issues are concerned. Currently, business organizations have to face up to the new norms of environmental targets, corporate social responsibility and other matters. Economic criteria used to take precedence over the views of fringe environmental

groups, but the media now define normality as one in which an endangered environment must be protected and form part of the criteria for competent management. In the early 1990s, oil company Shell came to media attention over a proposed deep-sea disposal of the Brent Spar oil rig, despite its eminently rational cost-benefit analysis, which attempted to bring environmental issues into the equation.

Along with these characteristics, academics are continually exercised about other qualitative variables in quantitative measures such as cost-benefit analysis. McQuail's two-dimensional framework for representing contrasting theoretical perspectives (media-centric vs society-centric, and culturalist vs materialist) is a helpful conceptual baseline from which to begin. It is shown in Figure 6.1.

RHETORIC VS REALITY

Large organizations rely on mass communication, particularly in the form of advertising. In addition to informing the public about products and services and inducing them to buy, advertisements communicate messages about the nature of the organization and its values, which may or may not reflect objective reality. Ind (1997) believes that public relations activity fulfils a similar strategic role to advertising, 'in that its function is to increase awareness and improve favourability, but loses out to advertising in its controllability'. He uses as an example the American Anti-slavery Society, one of the longest and oldest public relations campaigns, which was formed in 1833 and established its own newspapers, held public meetings, distributed pamphlets and lobbied state legislatures and the US Congress demanding action to abolish slavery. 'Even after the American Civil War, the society still campaigned for constitutional amendments and civil rights laws to protect the gains of the newly freed slave. This led to the passing of the 13th Amendment abolishing slavery.'

The word 'mass' therefore can be given positive, negative or undifferentiated associations depending on the political perspective adopted. For example, positive in socialist rhetoric sees the masses as a source of strength, while negative, when associated with the dictators of the 1930s, subscribes to individualistic and elitist cultural values. However, in a communication context it refers to a large, seemingly undifferentiated audience. This is essentially an asymmetrical stance, because message receivers had little chance to share their perceptions with the mass of other message receivers up until the new technology allowed, for example, chat rooms on the web.

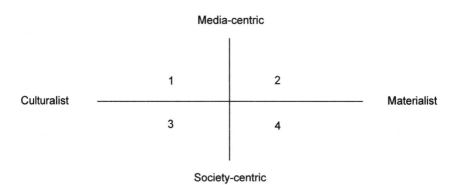

Figure 6.1 *Perspectives on media and society*

Source: McQuail (1994)

Key
Media-centric/society-centric: the media-centric/society-centric dimension contrasts approaches that focus on the media's own sphere of activity and see it as a primary mover in social change, as opposed to where the media are seen as reflecting wider political, social and economic forces. The other dimension takes a view which emphasizes culture and ideas as opposed to material forces and factors. McQuail sees these two dimensions as being independent. This allows for four different perspectives on media and society, and is a useful organizational barometer for media relations when planning responses to particularly sensitive issues.

Media culturist/media materialist: the corporate communication or business strategy of a firm at any particular moment or situation will influence the approach taken by the public relations planner. From a media/culturalist view, an organization might concentrate on the content and reception of media messages; for example, whether a public relations campaign to convince the public that the organization improved the environment was being received by active members of the green movement in the way the organization desired. A media/materialist approach, for example, would look at the role that technological developments such as the internet were having on the media channels available to the public relations programme. A society/culturalist approach offers less of an emphasis on the media itself than on its social role, particularly the role of the press in influencing social and political attitudes. Finally, a society/materialist perspective would see the media and its influence as deriving from economic and material conditions in society; this would be an extreme example of McQuail's quadrant.

MESSAGE MODELLING

A pluralistic, process approach to any strategic public relations endeavour inevitably involves the mass media at some point. There are a number of different models which help to show how it might inform the public relations manager of today's organization. These include:

- *The transmission model* – this model views communication as transmitting a fixed amount of information. The sequence of sender–message–channel–receiver is now seen as naive and is replaced by the sequence of events and voices in society, channel/communicator role, message, receiver, thereby recognizing that the mass media are not the originators of the message, but rather that they are relaying their account of a selection of events.
- *The ritual or expressive model* – the former model implies that there is an instrumental motive in the communication process, that the message is trying to achieve something. However, communication is sometimes seen as a form of ritual when it expresses sharing, participation, association, fellowship and the possession of a common faith. Many advertising campaigns exploit the mass media in this way, not transmitting information about the product or service but rather associating it with a supposedly shared value. For example, a butter product might be associated with factory-produced beer as representing traditional images of rural life and the country inn.
- *The publicity model* – this sees the sender as not attempting to transmit anything, but rather simply seeking to catch visual or oral attention. The public may see the media not so much as a source of information but as escapism from everyday reality. Many organizations find it possible to exploit this aspect of the mass media, especially organizations such as Greenpeace, who can provide exciting and attention-grabbing film footage such as a motor boat cutting across the bows of a Japanese trawler, which guarantees media attention.
- *The reception model* – this argues that any meaningful message is built up with signs whose meanings depend on choices made by the sender or encoder. Receivers or decoders are not of course obliged to accept the messages sent. They can put their own interpretation on what they receive and therefore a reception model is dependent on an encoding and decoding process by those involved in sending or receiving communication.

All organizations plan their relationship with the media as part of their overall public relations policy. Here it is not possible to proceed without some comment about the term 'public relations' and the dilemma in which the Chartered Institute of Public Relations finds itself in terms of its own identity and reputation. Public relations has acquired a pejorative association in the minds of many people because it has been perceived as being a process by which organizations attempt to conceal the truth about their activities behind a smokescreen. In political circles, a public relations practitioner has become a 'spin doctor' whose narrowly defined function is to deflect public criticism and to defend his or her masters or mistresses from public criticism. The shortened marketing acronym 'PR' for public relations is symbolic of this and, some argue, has added to the profession's status difficulties as it is often not regarded as a discipline based on reliable and valid empirical methodologies. Educators, therefore, usually avoid its use wherever possible, in the same way as they would not refer to CA for chartered accountancy.

THINK GLOBAL, ACT LOCAL

Some of the key issues affecting corporate strategy relate to globalization and the new technology, which have brought about the globalization of markets, the development of worldwide networks, a widening of membership for pressure groups and a broader analysis of competition. It therefore seems an almost pointless exercise to plan strategically in a chaotic environment in which the notion of managing risk appears by definition to be a misnomer. If the power of individual nation states to control national economies has become limited, the problems of a borderless world become more acute.

As most public relations practitioners know, campaigns have to be planned at the global level, but acted out at the local level. The importance of region states or areas is defined by some degree of economic logic which may lie within a nation state or cross-nation state boundaries. So, just as the relevance of the nation state is being called into question, it is apparent that the modern multinational is continuing to lose what was left of its national character. Reich (1990) gives the example of Whirlpool which now employs 43,500 people around the world, most of them non-American, in 45 countries. He points out that Texas Instruments does most of its research and development, design and manufacturing in East Asia. Reich showed that a company's most important competitive asset is the skills and cumulative learning of its workforce if it is equipped to compete in the global economy.

Jolly (1996) wrote that, as evidence of a global public relations strategy, a company must be able to demonstrate selective contestability and global resources. Selective contestability is where the corporation can contest any market it chooses to compete in, but can be selective about where it wishes to compete. It is prepared to contest any market should the opportunity arise and is constantly on the global lookout for such. In the chapter covering marketing communication we saw that such organizations represent potential new entrants in all global markets.

The corporation may have to bring its entire worldwide resources to bear on any competitive situation it finds itself in anywhere in the world. Customers know that they are dealing with a global player even if it is employing a local competitive formula. Thus global strategies are not standard product market strategies which assume that the world is a homogenous border-free marketplace. Nor are they just about global presence. If what the corporation does in one country has no relation to what it does in other countries that is no different from dealing with various domestic competitors. Finally, globalization is not just about large companies now that the internet makes it possible for small companies to trade worldwide.

TODAY'S FUTURE

The full potential impact of the internet cannot yet be assessed, but there is clearly strategic potential for using it as an information and transaction channel, for distributing news and for building communication channels. Web pages need to be constantly updated, which requires investment in multimedia expertise. The design and research aspects of managing an organization's worldwide website are offering growth potential for many public relations agencies and consultancies, albeit their use is increasingly complex in terms of corporate communication planning. The cliché, 'think global (big), act local (small)' is no longer enough unless evaluation stands up to the rigour of quantitative and qualitative audits across barriers of culture, language, traditions and beliefs.

New research techniques such as web analysis using tools like new generation eye-trackers to collect objective data are changing the face of promotional planning via 'saved time', IT talent and new challenges to creativity. However, in the management of press and other public relations deadlines and the creative public relations talent that goes into campaigning, the ever-changing demands of media law should never be underestimated. Areas in European law such as libel, copyright and intellectual property are critical to the underpinning of any public relations campaign or strategy. If an organization's reputation is to be protected, there must be respect for the spirit as well as the letter of the law. In the not too distant future, there is likely to emerge a rash of comprehensive and sophisticated books on the new technologies from mass communication specialists.

CAMPAIGN: ROYAL CARIBBEAN INTERNATIONAL, USA

Royal Caribbean International embarked on a campaign to raise port security to a national issue of equal importance to airport security, in the process positioning itself as a partner to the government in its quest to secure the United States. Additionally, the campaign positioned Royal Caribbean as a stakeholder partner to consumers, showcasing the safety innovations the company instituted to protect passengers. Port security regulations were subsequently imposed, a range of positive media placements was produced and the company's stock price soared along with increased cruising activity.

Challenge vs opportunity

Despite the creation of the Department of Homeland Security and the investment of billions of dollars by federal, state and local governments to better protect the country against those who wish to destroy it, a continuing sense of vulnerability prevailed.

Few scenarios frighten Americans more than the prospect of someone smuggling a nuclear weapon into the country through one of their 5,000-plus US port facilities. In a country that received more than 7 million pieces of container freight that year, such a scenario was no longer considered to be far-fetched, but was perceived as a realistic danger demanding complete attention.

However, the task of safeguarding US ports consistently found itself to be of secondary concern in the government's homeland security efforts, evidenced by the fact that only 5 per cent of incoming cargo was being inspected. The US government dedicated no money at all for seaports in its 2003 and 2004 budgets and, of the $5.4 billion the Coast Guard estimates it would cost to fully secure US ports, the Bush administration spent just $395 million.

At the same time, all sectors of the travel industry felt the impact caused by the ongoing threat of terrorism amidst an already depressed economy. Add the war in Iraq, the SARS outbreak, rising fuel prices and the Norwalk virus, and the US cruising sector experienced one of the most challenging business environments ever.

Research

It was imperative to illustrate that port security was not only being overlooked by many policymakers, but was also an issue that was critical to the success of the government's overall homeland security efforts. Key findings of subsequent research included:

- an estimated 212,000 vessels brought 7.3 million containers into the nation's ports each year;
- of the $827 billion of trade done with countries outside of North America, 95 per cent entered the country by ship;
- less than 5 per cent of containers entering US harbours were searched;
- funding for devices that could detect radioactive material had stalled; and
- disruption of activity at a major US port would have enormous economic implications, evidenced by events in the previous autumn when a 10-day strike by dock workers at Oakland and 28 other West Coast ports cost businesses $2 billion a day in lost sales.

Strategic plan

A strategic campaign governing four key principles was designed which would:

- make the case by educating key audiences and build heightened awareness of the critical importance of port security;
- elevate the expert by driving awareness and credibility of Royal Caribbean through ongoing dialogue with policymakers and influential media outlets;
- build a committed brand by positioning Royal Caribbean as a devoted leader in safeguarding the nation's ports, as well as a company strongly committed to protecting its customers in an environment where many have concerns about travel; and
- move the bottom line by building upon the re-energized, committed Royal Caribbean brand to drive towards stronger overall business growth.

Operational strategy

Meetings for Royal Caribbean with key policymakers in Washington, including the Department of Homeland Security, were secured. A speaking opportunity for Captain Bill Wright, Royal Caribbean's senior vice president of safety and security, at the prestigious McGraw-Hill Homeland Security Summit in Washington DC was arranged to build credibility. Further meetings between Royal Caribbean personnel and key journalists in Washington were organized to forge media/press relations and to increase the company's pedigree and showcase its commitment to the homeland security effort.

Evaluation outcomes

The perceived importance of port security as a national issue steadily increased. Federal regulations took effect by the end of the year, requiring more than 5,000 port facilities and 10,000 vessels to assess their potential vulnerability and develop plans to plug security holes, including establishing baggage, cargo and passenger screening similar to that at airports. Approved plans had to be put into place domestically and abroad by a certain date. Steering the issue of port security towards national prominence was Royal Caribbean. Fuelling the charge was a steady stream of media interviews, including an on-ship feature on CNBC touting Royal Caribbean's security prowess, and interviews with the likes of the *Wall Street Journal, Business Week, Washington Post,* and the *New York Times.*

Evidencing the success of the campaign, CNBC chief intelligence expert Chris Whitcomb said:

> Royal Caribbean and Celebrity Cruises (also owned by Royal Caribbean International) hosted 2.8 million travellers last year aboard 25 ships with no major incidents. In a world where terrorism is just one of many safety concerns, that seems a pretty remarkable achievement.

While driving home its key security messages to both the federal government and the US consumer, the strategic campaign also communicated the financial strength of the company and its leadership position within the cruising industry. On 1 November 2002, Royal Caribbean shares traded at $18.47. By 1 October 2003, that share price stood at $29.05. As noted in a 24 April *Investor's Business Daily* feature on the company, 'while most big airlines were awash in red ink in 2002, Royal Caribbean managed to grow its year-over-year earnings 21 per cent'. CNNfn thought so much of the company that it made it the 'stock of the day' on 7 April.

The campaign also helped to re-ignite confidence and interest in cruising among the US public, thereby helping to encourage a much talked about industry rebound. While other travel sectors struggle, cruising continues to thrive. Having emerged from a challenging travel environment, Royal Caribbean is perceived in key circles as the cruise brand leader.

REFLECTION

Based on the information provided:

i.   Which of McQuail's five media characteristics were important to American society in respect of cruising activity?
ii.   Which media perspective did Royal Caribbean International take when addressing the challenge of port security?
iii. Which of the four mass communication models described in the chapter appear to underpin the campaign and why?
iv.   Describe some of the issues and their potential consequences between the company and government as key stakeholder.
v.   Describe some of the factors necessary to retain corporate confidence through ongoing relations with other stakeholders such as customers and journalists.

7

Research methods: measures and motives

Most management disciplines that are well regulated and well regarded are founded in established practices that are rigorously researched. Given that public relations is a management discipline, the lack of a reliable, generic research base in public relations has been a hindrance to the profession. For example, measuring the effects of core strategic public relations programmes over time as a value-added corporate component of an organization, whether in profit or not-for-profit enterprises, demands both pure and applied research skills. It is not possible in a single chapter to offer a systematic exploration of all types of research and methods of evaluation, but some key concepts and approaches are described as an introduction to social science research as it relates to public relations theory and practice.

ART VS SCIENCE

A more scientific approach to evaluation is emerging based on developments from media studies, market research and more specifically from both audience and social psychology research tools such as MRIs, eye-trackers and other high-tech developments. These developments provide essential information for the justification of public relations budgets through quality assured evaluation of strategic public relations programmes. The Dozier model shown in Figure 7.1 provides a conceptual matrix by which practitioners can classify and report the impact of their activities.

Evaluation and research also play an increasingly important role in the underpinning of strategic public relations systems and processes through the systematic gathering, recording and analysing of data relating to image, identity, reputation and perception by all stakeholders having an interest in the success or development of an organization. These include research into such elements as advertising effectiveness, media efficacy and corporate image, both internally and externally.

As the sources of information grow and become more easily accessible (government statistics, business directories, specialist digests and pocket books, international data, specialized trade periodicals, internet databases, etc), public relations decision making improves all the time. Added to this is the better quality of industrial and other surveys, including attitude surveys, field surveys and interview techniques.

In successful companies, systems are constantly changing and so executives' knowledge and daily contact with operations, the marketplace

		Content of evaluation	
	Preparation	Dissemination	Impact
Individualistic	Communication activities prepared via application of internalized professional standards of quality	Dissemination of messages evaluated by reactions of mass media professionals	Impact of PR activities evaluated via subjective qualitative 'sense' of publics' reactions
Scientific	Communication activities prepared via application of scientifically derived knowledge of publics	Dissemination of messages evaluated by quantified measures of media usage of messages	Impact of PR activities evaluated via objective, quantitative measure of publics' reactions

Figure 7.1 *Content and method in evaluation*

Source: Dozier, in Grunig (1992)

and consultancies create an ever-evolving strategy formulation process. At public relations conferences and meetings, workshops and committees, people from competing companies, suppliers and customers talk to each other and in this way often learn about the first signs of significant developments in the tools and techniques available.

The implementation of a communication strategy is often not thought out until the business strategy has been adopted by a main board or other senior management. Implementation is then sometimes left to the tactics people without clear guidelines, with the result that top-down approaches often ignore the contribution that public relations makes to competitive advantage in a knowledge management economy.

At a strategic level, public relations affects the whole organization and so, inevitably, the involvement of all top management is crucial for success. At an operational or tactical level, awareness of public relations outcomes at the very least is crucial and needs to be coordinated and managed effectively, particularly at the point of decision making. Tactical communication decisions have to be seen to fit into corporate or business objectives and this requires corporate communication coordination at board level.

VALIDITY AND RELIABILITY

Experienced practitioners are only too familiar with the dangers inherent in allowing style and creativity to run away with the substance of the original brief and its message, not least when a campaign takes on a life of its own outside the remit of the strategic plan. With the internet having driven general awareness of the importance of sound information as a means of influencing group managements and their governance policies, the corporate communication industry finds itself revisiting post-war European precepts. In the 1960s, at the dawn of mass communication as we know it today, social scientists such as Otto Lerbinger and Albert J Sullivan (1965) published their now classic model of the four elements of communication: information, influence, impact and empathy. For many practitioners the internet is no different from collecting data by telephone, letter or fax, but it does facilitate the collection of data from larger groups of people and thus produce wider sampling.

The public relations industry has tended to rely on research developments from the United States and thus most of the principles which Europe now follows are deemed to be fairly universal, albeit with a clear caveat in terms of cultural similarities and differences alongside national and professional ethical protocols. Most practitioners are familiar with the advantages and disadvantages of internet-based research methods, not least in terms of environmental scanning or monitoring of media and other information sources. These secondary research methods are informal and can support formal research methods which require inferential reasoning, both quantitative and qualitative.

The most popular use of online communication is ethnography, where online discussion groups can reveal patterns of social relationships even though participation is taking place in a virtual space via chat rooms or video conferencing. Another use is gathering qualitative research via focus groups, and here the advantages and disadvantages compared to face-to-face, including personal interviewing, are about equal. The other key use is online social surveys by e-mail and web surveys which can be used to supplement traditional questionnaires. This is the area attracting most government interest as a means by which democracy can be sustained via the ballot box. Bryman (2004) identifies the critical differences between synchronous and asynchronous methods of data collection, the former being in real time, eg online in a chat room; the latter where there is an online time lag between the parties which is of unknown duration. This has critical implications for long-term public relations planning.

Some of the most interesting developments in online communication are the integrative approaches being taken by large organizations to teleworking, which concerns itself with both top-down measures of effectiveness and efficiency as well as bottom-up concerns for operational competencies. The implications for the public relations and communication industry are significant. Illegems and Verbeke (2004) demonstrated that broader strategic considerations, beyond immediate impact on the bottom line, do influence the choice to adopt the practice of telework or remote working, because teleworking requires setting clear performance objectives and measures to a sophisticated degree 'as business and society becomes increasingly IT capable' (p 333). Clearly 'the study of telework in multinational enterprises may be particularly important... to assess the impact of location and activity scope of affiliates within a single firm on the adoption of this practice' (p 332). Illegems and Verbeke cite AT&T, Signa, Eli Lilly, Hewlett Packard and Notel as just five of some 1,000 global companies adopting teleworking. Figure 7.2 offers two perspectives on telework which will influence future organizational communication strategies.

BALANCED SCORECARD

The balanced scorecard as a tool for in-house communication practitioners is only helpful in facilitating and controlling public relations performance measurements for management if it is applied as a strategy implementation

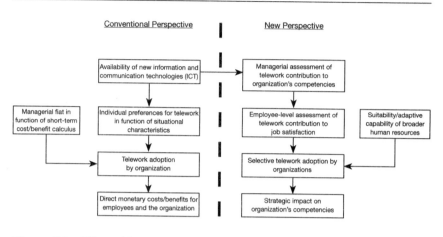

Figure 7.2 *Teleworking*

Source: Illegems and Verbeke (2004)

tool and not just as a performance measurement system at particular moments in time. As Braam and Nijssen (2004) found when exploring the performance effects of using the balanced scorecard in Holland, 'mechanistic use without a clear link to corporate strategy will hinder performance and may even decrease it' (p 344) and that the way it is used is important when translated from strategy into action; see Figure 7.3.

NARRATIVE METHODS

Many successful public relations programmes, including some of those to be found in this book, tell a story. Boje (2001) argues that a story is an account of incidents or events but, 'narrative comes after and adds plot and coherence to the storyline'. Philosophers such as Boje and postmodernists such as Jacques Derrider are exercised about the reliability and validity of analysis using story deconstruction. While the public relations industry recognizes the inevitable bias in any story rolled out in a public relations programme, it also recognizes that deconstructional analysis has a place in case study writing, the development of objectives, data collection, drafting a case, testing and revising. However, in the broader sense of public relations as public affairs, cultural considerations and ethical dilemmas, the following eight story deconstruction guidelines (Boje, 2001, adapted from Boje and Dennehy, 1993) can produce useful pointers to forward planning in terms of the acknowledgement of sensitivities and the identification of potential problems or issues ahead (see pp 109–10).

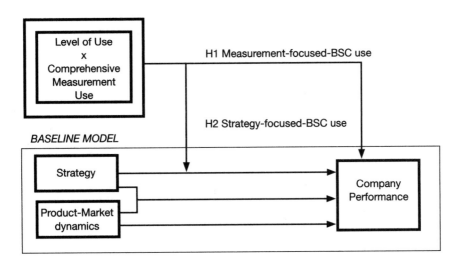

Figure 7.3 *Balanced scorecard application*

Source: Braam and Nijssen model, adapted from Kaplan and Norton (2001)

Key
H1: Measurement-focused-BSC use, ie the multiplication of the intensity or level of use by the usage of BSC as a comprehensive performance measurement system, will be positively related to company performance. *H2:* strategy-focused-BSC use, ie the moderator effect of measurement-focused-BSC use on strategy, will be positively related to company performance.

Deconstruction guidelines

1. *Duality search.* Make a list of any bipolar terms, any dichotomies that are used in the story. Include the term even if only one side is mentioned. For example, in male-centred and/or male-dominated organization stories, men are central and women are marginal others. One term mentioned implies its partner.
2. *Reinterpret the hierarchy.* A story is one interpretation or hierarchy of an event from one point of view. It usually has some form of hierarchical thinking in place. Explore and reinterpret the hierarchy (eg in duality terms how one dominates the other) so you can understand its grip.
3. *Reveal voices.* Deny the authority of the one voice. Narrative centres marginalize or exclude. To maintain a centre takes enormous energy. What voices are not being expressed in this story? Which voices are subordinate or hierarchical to other voices (eg, who speaks for the trees)?

4. *Other side of the story.* Stories always have two or more sides. What is the other side of the story (usually marginalized, under-represented, or even silent)? Reverse the story, by putting the bottom on top, the marginal in control, or the back stage up front. For example, reverse the male centre, by holding a spotlight on its excesses until it becomes a female centre in telling the other side; the point is not to replace one centre with another, but to show how each centre is in a constant state of change and disintegration.

5. *Deny the plot.* Stories have plots, scripts, scenarios, recipes and morals. Turn these around (move from romantic to tragic or comedic to ironic).

6. *Find the exception.* Stories contain rules, scripts, recipes and prescriptions. State each exception in a way that makes it extreme or absurd. Sometimes you have to break the rules to see the logic being scripted in the story.

7. *Trace what is between the lines.* Trace what is not said. Trace what is the writing on the wall. Fill in the blanks. Storytellers frequently use 'you know that part of the story'. Trace what you are filling in. With what alternative way could you fill it in (eg trace to the context, the back stage, the between, the intertext)?

8. *Resituate.* The point of doing 1 to 7 is to find a new perspective, one that resituates the story beyond its dualisms, excluded voices or singular viewpoint. The idea is to reauthor the story so that the hierarchy is resituated and a new balance of views is attained. Restory to remove the dualities and margins. In a resituated story there are no more centres. Restory to script new actions.

INTERTEXTUALITY ANALYSIS

Clearly, one area that is of particular significance to public relations practitioners is the way that press releases are written and designed to be read by different audiences. It is therefore useful to understand a little about intertextuality analysis so as to appreciate how each story is 'informed by other stories that the writer or reader has heard or read and their respective cultural contexts'. Boje believes that the narrative analysis of novels can be applied to organizational narratives as well, namely textual productivity, social and historical intertextual networks, intertextual distribution and consumption, intertextuality and carnival – what Boje describes as 'the theatrical resolve... to render various class, race, gender distinctions harmonious and therefore hegemonic with the commonsense legitimation of corporate texts, including strategy, identity and harmonious rationales' (p 76). Figure 7.4 suggests historical and social questions in intertextual analysis.

Global social contexts

Precedent texts			Anticipated texts
	• Whose social identities get constituted? • Who has access to being included in the text? • Who does the text quote? • Who speaks for whom? • What institutions commission the text?	• Whose conventions (genres, styles and types) does the text incorporate? • Who is the text distributed to for consumption? • Who are the audiences this text is designed to be interpreted and read by?	
	• How are parts of other texts incorporated into the text (quoted or interpreted)? • How are various stories incorporated? • What is the time and place of each utterance? • What are the footprints of the author?	• What is selected as newsworthy for target audiences? • What are the 'common sense' or 'insider' terms? • What are the parodies, ironies and metaphorization? • What interpretative matrix does the author construct for readers to consume?	

Local contexts

Figure 7.4 *Historicity and social questions for intertextual analysis*

Source: Boje (2001)

Another key method of storytelling analysis out of the eight offered by Boje is theme analysis. Inductive theme analysis is popular among some public relations research agencies in their search for patterns, particularly of cultural meaning based on taxonomies of similarities and differences. For creatives in a global context, awareness of basic narrative themes is likely to prove beneficial in the future. In the taxonomy shown in Figure 7.5, four types of narrative are considered: bureaucratic, quest, chaos and postmodern.

Given that the sequence of public relations objectives will normally include informational objectives, motivational objectives and behavioural objectives (Stacks, 2002), narrative methods for communication and public relations research play an increasingly significant part in qualitative research.

In telling stories, an attempt is often being made to persuade through simple or straightforward explanation. With the popularization of science and technology, even generalizations must be based on clear, impartial evidence. Illustrations often contribute to clarity, with television and new media excelling in the speed at which they produce diagrams for news and current affairs programmes. Even when announcing a medical breakthrough or presenting topical issues such as nuclear energy, accuracy and clarity in reporting relies on the judicious use of language in its cultural context. Barrass (2002) reminds us that, although scientists and engineers are being asked to write well these days, many technical terms have additional meanings in everyday use and cites the words 'allergy',

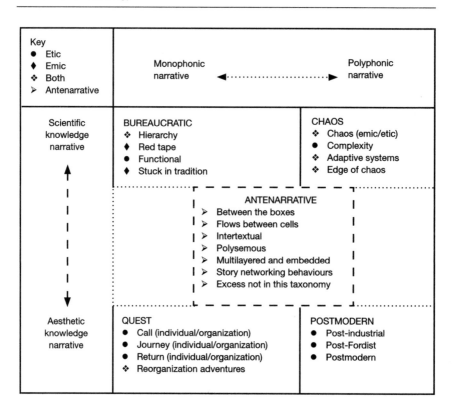

Figure 7.5 *Basic narrative themes*

Source: Boje (2001)

'neurotic' and 'subliminal' as examples, with the reminder that scientific and technical evidence must ensure that such words are used 'in the restricted scientific sense' (p 59). Narrative methods must never deflect from consistency and predictability (reliability) or from validity which challenges our perceptions both culturally and psychologically during the collection and measurement of data.

PR AS A SOCIAL SCIENCE

The public relations and communication industry relies on interdisciplinary and multidisciplinary research methodologies in the conduct of social research, including quantitative and qualitative theories, epistemology, ontology, the impact of values and the practical considerations of each factor. In a complex web, a crossover between market research and communication research can occur at any point in the choice of method, in the formulation of research design and data collection technique, in the implementation of data collection and in the analysis, interpretation and conclusions reached around that data.

A stakeholder approach clarifies the boundaries in that the quantitative and qualitative research strategies for collecting marketing communication data will address issues specifically related to the needs of customers, suppliers and buyers/producers. This is true whether the research design is experimental, cross-sectional, longitudinal, comparative or survey research on a single case study. Even with the development of value-added public relations to the bottom line via integrated marketing communication models, the strategic elements are straightforward, particularly in respect of sampling, both probability sampling (random sampling) and non-probability sampling (non-random sampling). Although market-related public relations is deemed to dominate in terms of fee income around consumer products compared to fee income to the public relations industry emanating from corporate, environmental and governmental areas, the impact and often negative criticism of the industry is felt less because it has little or fewer social and political implications. This is particularly relevant when measuring public relations campaigns and communication programmes, such as surveys of levels of awareness or related attitudes, when measuring audience reception or measures associated with changes in behaviour, eg the behaviour of managers following an internal communication audit and corporate governance initiatives. The range of other stakeholders such as shareholders, educators, media opinion leaders, churches and state may be appropriate targets for the selling of a product or service but, in terms of public relations theory, selling is usually a one-way process (information) not a two-way process (communication).

Population classification systems may rely on research lists such as Mosaic, which is based on census data in the UK but also includes other data sources to produce of system of 11 groups, which includes Urban Intelligence and Rural Isolation. Other geo-demographic systems include The Acorn Consumer classification with five groups: wealthy achievers, urban prosperity, comfortably off, moderate means and hard pressed. These have been adapted to serve the classification needs of specific markets such as investors and financial markets.

Theory can of course emerge from the collection and analysis of data, and qualitative research is often applied in the testing of theory ahead of data collection. However, multi-strategy research requires considerable research experience, skill and training and the ability to handle the outcomes which can be planned or unplanned, qualitative or quantitative. Although this book is not a 'how to' book and so does not instruct the reader in how to carry out quantitative methodologies such as bivariate analysis, multivariate analysis or statistical significance methods, nor qualitative methods such as interviewing, surveys or participant observation, a chapter on research would be remiss without mentioning the software package, SPSS for Windows. This is the most widely used package of computer software for analysing data because it saves time and is fairly easy to learn. Most public relations postgraduate programmes include training in it, or if they don't they should do so, because experience of SPSS is necessary at research planning and public relations programme design stage, where it is particularly important for coding or labelling data or units of analysis and the coding frame in respect of the coding of open questions. In content analysis, coding schedules are produced as forms on which all the data about an item being coded is entered and preserved. There are now statutory research ethical governance and regulation rules which must be adhered to in the UK and these underpin the CIPR's code of conduct and ethical statements.

CAMPAIGN: MARRIOTT HOTEL GROUP, INDONESIA

On 5 August 2003, a bomb exploded at the Marriott Hotel in Jakarta's business district. Rumours circulated of al-Qaeda terrorist connections, tourism was threatened, hotel occupancy plummeted overnight, and anxiety skyrocketed among the business community. Decisive action was needed to curb growing insecurities among the public, tourists and the business community.

Indo Pacific was appointed by the Jakarta Governor a few days after the Marriott bombing to establish a media centre to serve as a focus for incoming and outgoing information. This centre received praise from media and officials alike for providing a central coordination hub and assisting in minimizing the damage to Indonesia's reputation caused by unverified and inaccurate information.

Challenge vs opportunity

The blast at the Marriott, which killed 12 and injured almost 150, came two days before the verdict in the trial of a key suspect in the Bali bombing, resulting in speculation of a conspiracy. The bombing heightened fears that Islamic militants would continue to target foreign investors and tourists.

After the bombing tragedy in Bali eight months earlier, the international media descended on Jakarta to confirm whether al-Qaeda was operating in Indonesia. Indonesians felt their image and culture, as a predominantly Muslim country, were under attack internationally. Negative articles about how Indonesia handled terrorism steadily increased.

After the Bali bombing, uncertainty was exacerbated by the unavailability of a central coordination point for media. Contradictory statements were released from different parties. There was an urgent need for consistent coordinated messages and an integrated flow of information on the response of government officials, Islamic leaders, diplomats and the business community.

Research

Despite the unexpected context of crisis, the agency used lessons learnt from their handling of the media centre after the Bali bombing. They needed to determine the most strategic communication tools to reach a broad audience quickly and effectively and develop key messages that would contribute to restoring Indonesia's reputation. Spokespersons and officials most in demand by national and international media were identified.

Strategic plan

Given the time constraints, the agency would need to implement two fundamental activities simultaneously. The first would be to open the media centre at another hotel on 10 August 2004 to serve as a source of continuous updates and a central meeting point for media. The second was to build a network of government officials, journalists, religious leaders, diplomats and other resource people, and briefing them on how to communicate key messages effectively.

The objectives were to:

- control damage to Indonesia's reputation internationally by communicating steps being taken by the authorities;
- anticipate potential issues that may arise and provide credible first-hand information to international and national media on the authorities' efforts against terrorism;
- utilize international and national media by restoring the confidence of foreign investors and tourists, gaining support from Indonesian citizens in countering terrorism, and explain the role of Islam in modern Indonesia and the concept of *jihad* as distinct from terrorism.

Continuity planning

- Marriott would continue business operations as normal with foreign/ domestic investors and the business community, and it would maintain investment with active support from the authorities.
- The positive steps being taken by Indonesian officials would be presented to international and national media.
- Balanced news stories about security would be provided along with regular updates for the public on how Indonesia was handling security.
- International concerns about terrorism would never be taken lightly and information from government officials would remain transparent at all times.
- The confidence of citizens and foreign visitors in Indonesia's ability to handle security issues would have to be maintained while carrying out daily activities as usual, albeit with heightened vigilance.

Key messages

These were that the Indonesian authorities were committed to cracking down on those with terrorist links by working quickly to catch the perpetrators; Indonesia remains safe for business and tourism; and that bomb attacks are not only carried out by Muslims and indeed most of the victims were Muslims.

Operational strategy

The communication channels and vehicles included the establishment of a noticeboard outside the media centre displaying 24-hour contact numbers, schedule of guest speakers at twice daily media briefings, media announcements and updates, contact information for embassies and other resources. Invitations were faxed to all media on daily briefings, and the Indo Pacific website was used to provide transcripts of all media briefings in English and Indonesian for global media to download. Immediately following the bombing, meetings were held between the Jakarta Governor and Indo Pacific to establish a triangular cooperation between the Jakarta provincial administration, Jakarta Police and the Jakarta International Hotel Association (JIHA).

All internal and external communications originated from the media centre. Twice-daily media briefings were held with scheduled speakers, including representatives from the police, Governor's office, security firms, chambers of commerce, religious organizations and hospitals. The ministers of foreign affairs, tourism, and politics and security also addressed the media. Implementation focused on internal relations, which involved eliciting commitment of the three involved parties to the media centre, designed to run for two weeks during the critical recovery period, providing standby bilingual simultaneous interpreters and transcripts, and encouraging availability of the Governor and other spokespersons while ensuring transparency at all times.

Media relations activities included:

- updating national and international media on topics of daily briefings;
- accommodating requests and input from media and other interested parties;
- complying with media deadlines by immediately providing transcripts and notes of Q&A sessions;
- posting bilingual transcripts to facilitate media access online; and
- providing information on different angles for each issue (business, religious, security, victim status, tourism) to accommodate different media agendas.

Government and other party relations involved daily coordination with three initiating parties, and personal approaches and lobbying of the Minister of Political and Security Affairs, Indonesian Police, Nahdlatul Ulama and Muhammadiyah (first and second largest Islamic groups), national and international chambers of commerce, and other front-liners.

There was limited time to establish a media centre or to set up logistics and telecommunications capabilities. Sudden and frequent changes in schedules of key spokespersons required replacement speakers when necessary, and the varying demands of local and international media proved a challenge requiring constant adjustment to schedules.

Evaluation outcomes

Over 120 journalists representing 45 national and international media attended the media centre's first briefing at three hours' notice. There was continued high attendance throughout the two weeks and coverage by international media included Associated Press, Reuters, CNN and the BBC. Coverage of key messages by media produced balanced news stories, with over 140 articles in the Indonesian media being generated by the media centre within two weeks. Resolution and handling of all recorded media enquiries were complete in time for the media centre's closure. The media centre had maintained its reputation as the primary source of next-day edition stories and headlines, even providing a scoop on the government's plan to issue an anti-terror law.

Afterwards, the leading Indonesian daily, *Kompas,* reported that the media centre had made journalists' jobs easier and provided a forum for the direct flow of assistance to victims from key sources, eg Ministry of Social Affairs and charismatic Muslim cleric Abdullah Gymnastiar. It provided an early public warning of another possible attack on Indonesia's Independence Day and contributed to the development of the public perception that Indonesia was more prepared to accept and deal with terrorism on its soil. The rupiah maintained its value against the US dollar (Rp 8,953 – March 2003, Rp 8,889 – September, Rp 8,965 – December) while hotel occupancy only dropped for a few days and returned to normal within several weeks. The Governor announced plans to establish a new crisis centre to deal with bombing attacks and natural disasters, and the Minister of Tourism appointed Indo Pacific to visit Australia to explain the Indonesian post-bombing political and social situation.

REFLECTION

Based on the information provided:

i.   Critically appraise the content and method of agency evaluation through the classic Dozier 1992 model.
ii.   Given the criticality of the internet to business performance, what role, if any, might teleworking and balanced scorecards have played during the crisis?
iii. In the news stories that emerged, which of the practical guidelines were likely to prove most useful?
iv.   In the aftermath of the crisis, which historical and/or social issues should form part of future public relations campaign objectives?
v.   The core activity of any continuity planning is corporate communication, so how did Marriott's government relations help rather than hinder?

8

The ethical dimension: a moral imperative

Increasingly, communication experts and public relations practitioners find themselves involved in mediation, conflict resolution and relationship or personal communication development programmes. Christians and Traeber (1997) identified a broad-based ethical theory of communication which transcends cultures and the world of mass media. They believed it could be accepted by society as a whole and that organizations would find it possible to adopt and adapt it to form the basis of organizational codes. Christians and Traeber demonstrate that, 'certain ethical protonorms – above all truth telling, commitment to justice, freedom in solidarity and respect for human dignity – are validated as core values in communications in different cultures'. They conclude that, 'we are in search of the ultimate and unconditional characteristics of human life, from which the meaning of human actions can be derived. Communication is one such act'.

The development and pretesting of the means for achieving ethical objectives through research is one factor in the developing assessment framework suggested earlier in this book. Pretests are 'reliable estimates of how programme strategies will work', say Kirban and Jackson (1990).

They warn of the danger of operating by instinct instead of employing creative and artistic decisions based on research. A generation ago, Ehling (1985) warned that public relations would be incomplete and flawed with technician behaviour replacing management-level functioning if it were not based on research. He believed that public relations is:

> a decision-making, problem-solving activity essentially concerned with selecting and specifying end states (goals, objectives) to be attained by an organization or group and with developing, programming and implementing efficient and effective means (courses of action, strategies) for attaining or accomplishing the desired end states.

In 1978, the worldwide public relations industry produced the Mexican statement, emanating from an international meeting of the same year, stating that public relations is the art and social science of analysing trends, predicting their consequences, counselling organization leaders and implementing planned programmes of action which serve both the organization's and the public's interests. While key words in the original CIPR definition were 'planned', 'mutual' and 'publics', in the Mexican statement keywords are 'research', 'analysing', 'counselling' and 'both'. The Mexican definition excludes knee-jerk reactions to environmental influences and indicates that public relations involves an advisory function which in any democracy requires a clear ethical stance. Public relations professionals, whether in-house or outsourced, give advice to senior managers in organizations and emphasize the need to serve the public interest, even where that term is ill-defined.

PR VS PROPAGANDA

It is essential to distinguish corporate public relations from propaganda, because public perception often confuses the two concepts. Elliott (1975) defines propaganda as:

> statements of policy or facts, usually of a political nature, the real purpose of which is different from their apparent purpose. In this sense propaganda existed before the twentieth century, but its importance has increased in an age when communication is easier and when it is more useful to influence ordinary people. The term is used to describe a statement which is believed to be insincere or untrue, and designed to impress the public rather than to reach the truth or to bring about a genuine understanding between opposing governments or parties. People do not usually admit that they are issuing propaganda, and the word is much misused. Propaganda by one's own government or political party is described as a policy statement or as part

of its news service; genuine approaches and statements of policy by another government or party are frequently dismissed as mere propaganda.

This is as true today as when it was written.

In order to succeed, public relations must be transparent, free from bias and demonstrate a two-way dynamic process where the aim is mutual understanding of the facts even if there is no subsequent agreement on policy or ideology. Organizations often need to respond to unfavourable criticism. Jefkins (1993) argued for an anatomy of public relations based on the transfer process, which shows an organization converting four negative states into positive ones, whereby hostility is converted into sympathy; prejudice to acceptance; apathy to interest; and ignorance to knowledge.

ETHICAL EVALUATION

Even within the UK National Health Service (NHS), which is held in such high esteem, there is still a lack of systematic ethical evaluation. The principles of the Declaration of Helsinki are relevant to the NHS or any organization in terms of efficacy, skill and reputation. The moral principles from the Declaration demonstrate that:

- any enquiry involving human participants should not occur unless aims and methods can achieve the stated and appropriate goals;
- any risk associated with human enquiry should always be proportional to its potential benefits, remembering that the interests and rights of individual participants should not be ignored in the name of the public good;
- individuals should not participate in human inquiry without their consent, after they have been given adequate information about the aims, methods, potential benefits, risks and other practical implications for them of their participation; and
- the confidentiality of individuals who participate in research should always be respected, irrespective of whether their participation is direct or indirect.

The moral importance of independent evaluation stems from the potential for researchers themselves to underestimate the problems associated with new campaign proposals. The best intentions can lead to improper aims and methods, along with unrecognized conflicts of interest. In the NHS, regional ethics committees are now well established and advise universities and individuals in every part of the UK.

However, an important aspect of sound ethical practice is transparency, which can be problematic in covert observation that may nevertheless be in the best interests of the public good, eg sociological research into activities of criminals. As Bryman states (2004, p 520), the political dimensions of research are concerned with issues to do with the role and exercise of power, which links to a society or culture's value system, an increasingly complex issue in global ethical decision making for international organizations. Thus, today's leading corporate public relations directors and outsourced advisers and consultants are coaches, helping to create learning organizations. In the United States, they are referred to as 'counsellors'. They work with CEOs to balance risk during change and conflict by both goal setting (mission) and vision (statements) in line with sustainable development and continuity planning. Marketing publicity and promotion contribute to this in a creative but time-controlled manner in the selling of product and service.

In the UK, the government was concerned that there would never be enough capital to develop Qinetiq, the research arm of the Ministry of Defence. So, in Spring 2006, it was floated on the London Stock Exchange, with only a 25 per cent share remaining with the Ministry of Defence and 75 per cent being held by private equity groups and other stakeholders. Journalist Andrew Gilligan wrote in the *London Evening Standard* (24 January 2006): 'if the company comes to be ruled by the bottom line, the risk is that Qinetiq will rest on its evaluation work and its already proven technologies, and some of that creativity will fade'. He explains how Qinetiq is:

> a national treasure house of intellectual property and scientific endeavour that has until now been used to enrich the nation rather than its own senior management. Few other major governments, certainly not the Americans, have taken a similar route with their defence research bodies. Then there is the prospect of conflicts of interest.

There are key communication implications for different styles of corporate governance. In the West, most countries are divided into three groups, having monistic, dualistic and pluralistic concepts of their corporations based on their nation's history, economy, politics and culture. With emerging technological convergence, the level of skill involved in reassuring a country's public while retaining core cultural norms is a challenge to business leaders and their core communication strategies. There is no reason why strategic thinking cannot be both logical and creative so long as it is ethical. Table 8.1 offers a rational thinking versus generative thinking perspective.

Long-term public relations campaigns depend on generative thinking and diplomacy in the building of relations with governments, financial

Table 8.1 *Rational thinking vs generative thinking*

	Rational	*Generative*
Emphasis on	Logic over creativity	Creativity over logic
Cognitive style	Analytical	Intuitive
Reasoning follows	Formal, fixed rules	Informal, variable rules
Nature of reasoning	Computational	Imaginative
Direction of reasoning	Vertical	Lateral
Value placed on	Consistency and rigour	Unorthodoxy and vision
Reasoning hindered by	Incomplete information	Adherence to current ideas
Assumption about reality	Objective, (partially) knowable	Subjective, (partially) creatable
Decisions based on	Calculation	Judgement
Metaphor	Strategy as science	Strategy as art

Source: de Wit and Meyer (1999)

institutions such as the World Bank and non-governmental organizations (NGOs).

A current project managed by the UK government's Department for International Development is using the perspective of strategic communication to fight poverty through a long-term public relations process, which includes information dissemination, events, promotion of the concept itself, consultation, awareness raising, workshops, seminars and campaigns. Named the 'Poverty Reduction Strategy', the global project's public relations team argues that communication intervention is one of the major elements of their poverty reduction objective because participation of key stakeholders is one of the major characteristics in terms of partnership and country ownership during preparation and implementation. It recognizes that one of the critical elements of a strategic communication intervention is that communication activities are planned, designed, organized and implemented in a coherent, strategic manner. The strategic issues involve:

- identifying the sender of information for each communication activity;
- message development;
- confidence and trust;
- packaging the information;
- timing;

- sustaining momentum;
- quality and accuracy of information;
- follow-up and linkages;
- culture;
- language;
- attitudes and behaviour;
- institutional issues such as coordination and collaboration with other government and NGO departments and agencies;
- capacity-building; and
- costing.

Some of the structural impediments to participation and country ownership are found in the underlying political culture, but access to information can also be a problem.

An important ethical definition is offered by the United Nations Development Programme and states that:

> access to information is not only about promoting and protecting rights to information but is equally concerned with promoting and protecting communication (use of information) to voice one's views, to participate in democratic processes that take place at all levels (community, national, regional and global) and to set priorities for action. (UNDP, 2003, p 3)

Communication within and between the key stakeholder groups are mapped as a framework for strategic communication, none of which is homogenous; see Figure 8.1.

An institutional theory perspective of strategic management underpins this corporate communication project using the process of isomorphism in the expectation that most stakeholders experience similar social expectations even where disparities of wealth are so marked.

The dynamic global environments in which organizations operate require multidimensional approaches to strategic management. From early military models to transaction cost economic models, global markets and e-commerce are reshaping strategic management theory and practice. Competition analysis now incorporates allowances, cooperative agreements and entrepreneurship with the business model used and abused more widely than ever before. Public relations practitioners are central to an organization's strategy in matching company plans to the competitive environment with the organization's resources and capabilities.

Media stories on the troubles at Enron, Parmalot, MCI World Com and others have brought the issue of strategic management into sharp focus, giving some celebrity CEOs iconic status, while covering reams of newsprint about the role of expertise or lack of it, and personal and

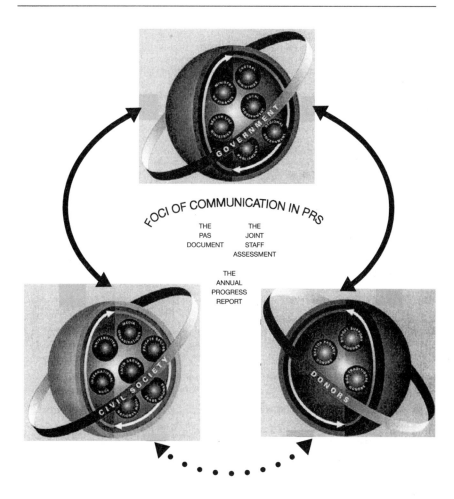

Figure 8.1 A framework for analysing strategic communication in the poverty reduction strategy campaign

Source: DfID/The World Bank, in Mozammel and Odugbemi (2005)

professional qualities essential to organizational success in the longer term. Economic and environmental pressures have once again raised the profile of corporate public relations and corporate communication's role in the boardroom as firms monitor and track micro and macro economies and environments in the face of threats to resources and prices. Annual reports, company statements and sound-bite clichés are scrutinized for efficiency and effectiveness from a social perspective. Opinion formers look to see if CEOs are committed to long-term sustainability of their organizations and have clear direction and tactics based on agreed behavioural and ethical standards. Their public relations advisers are supported in this role by the organization's own codes of conduct and ethics statements, as well as that of the professional Institute.

The CIPR operates a code of professional conduct with disciplinary powers to which all members agree to adhere. The Professional Practices Committee of the Institute has occasion to handle complaints brought against members of the Institute who are thought to be in breach of the Code. In regard to the supply of public relations services, the Code emphasizes that honest and proper regard for the public interest, reliable and accurate information, and never misleading clients, employers and other professionals about the nature of representation or what can be competently delivered or achieved, are vital components of robust professional advice. A full Review of the Code is available to all on www.cipr.co.uk.

CAMPAIGN: THE RUSSIAN PUBLIC RELATIONS ASSOCIATION

The Russian Public Relations Association (RPRA) was established in July 1991. RPRA is the first Russian professional and non-commercial organization that unites Russian and foreign public relations specialists. At the moment there are 72 company and individual members in Moscow, and 8 regional branches, with public relations agencies from Estonia and Kazakhstan. RPRA has established close cooperation with international public relations organizations and so recognizes and follows the codes of ethics and working practices established by the Confédération Européenne de Relations Publiques (CERP), the International Public Relations Association (IPRA) and the Chartered Institute of Public Relations (CIPR).

Consolidation of efforts of individual operators in the public relations market to solve issues in the sector was critical, and this could only be achieved through developing the public relations industry infrastructure supported by comprehensive and ongoing training programmes. It required protection of the public relations industry interests in general and each of its subjects in particular, plus the introduction of professional and ethical standards in practice, as well as control of their protocols. The latter identified development of HR potential in the public relations industry and introducing university and postgraduate education in public relations.

When the term 'public relations' or 'PR' appeared in Russia's vocabulary it became a popular expression, but there was little understanding of the term and the role public relations plays in a modern business environment. Most of the population's knowledge of public relations is limited to recognition of its role within political conflicts over the last 10 years.

In the past, Russians have been heard to claim that they are the best-read nation in the world, due in part to the fact that Russia is home to one of the largest domestic and international press corps in the world. It has 3,000 broadcasting companies and over 33,000 print media outlets, with a large percentage based in Moscow and St Petersburg. Russia's 145 million population is spread over a wide territory and relies heavily on the media for information. Media relations is therefore the core instrument for political and business communication.

Most Russian journalists were trained in Soviet schools and, when they went to work, were told what to write. Communist reformer Mikhail Gorbachev introduced his 'glasnost', or openness, policy in the mid-1980s, believing that a free press would expose social and political evils and generate public support for change. Journalists enthusiastically turned the late-Soviet media into a wild free-for-all that was intensely interesting, if not always professional. But somehow, during the harsh market reforms of the past decade, much of the media has lapsed into a state of political obedience and commercial venality, with political public relations specialists suffering the consequences of unprofessional practices within the industry.

The RPRA now commissions regular surveys of the public relations market to track core industry indicators. The RPRA's role includes conducting educational workshops and round tables for different focus groups, including their members, media representatives, universities/students, business leaders and other business and international groups. A top Russian public relations and communication agency was contracted to analyse the environment; it was recognized that building an entire communications industry from scratch would be a gigantic task.

Challenge vs opportunity

During the long Soviet era, there was no public relations or integrated marketing communication in Russia, so companies did not have to compete for the attention and preference of a stakeholder group or customer. The market was poor and always in deficit, so that any goods of any quality always sold. Second, since all means of communication were state-owned, any word in any publication was read and interpreted as a direct statement from the Kremlin and any product or brand information was considered to be 100 per cent truthful.

As a result, both communicators and their target audiences had no understanding of even the most basic notions of democratic, stakeholder communication. When the market began to develop and public relations companies started to compete, the first and easiest solution was therefore to buy media and simply extend advertising to non-advertising pages. Placing these promotional materials was at that time the main business of the newly-formed Russian public relations agencies. 'Zakazukha', or bought-and-paid-for news articles, became a standard practice in the Russian media. This is still, unfortunately, very prevalent among many non-Western agencies, with a wide range of practices. These include long-term, multi-area agreements with publishing houses, TV and radio companies. 'Information cooperation agreements' on the volume of advertising and non-advertising (advertorial) coverage the company is to receive over a period of time, say a year, are legal, binding agreements and are very common practice. When the company is developing, say, an integrated marketing strategy and budget, these kinds of contracts are planned and signed with the media with the best outreach to the target audience.

The same applies if the company executes its integrated marketing strategy via an agency. The agency usually agrees with the media not only on the advertising space, but on 'editorial' space as well. If the client is running a one-off campaign or needs to add to the media-buying plan, it goes to the editor to pay for extra 'editorial' space. This is usually paid to the editor in cash and costs a company less than paying via contract. A cheaper, though less reliable practice, is to pay the journalist, but sometimes a company finds that an editor drops an article from an issue because she or he didn't get a share of the cash payment.

Some publications somehow mark their advertorial space. Sometimes the page is marked with 'placed as advertising' or the whole page is of a different colour, or the font is different. However, many publications try to make this distinction minimal and most of the readers do not realize which material is paid for and which is not. Also, as public relations and journalism are synonyms of shameless manipulation and promoting everything for a price, the general population does not believe in objective or balanced coverage.

Research

Clearly the negative reputation of public relations in Russia had to be addressed, with the causes and incidents of unprofessional practices, including illiteracy, identified. It was necessary to draw the attention of state officials to the importance of developing good public relations practices in Russia and to establish trust in public relations agencies as professionals in solving communication issues and dilemmas.

Partnerships across all interested parties needed to be built.

Operational strategy

A 12-month programme of positive action events based around three major annual international public relations platforms was devised to rebuild the reputation of public relations in Russia and to raise practices to international levels. These were PR days in Moscow (February 2003), Baltic PR Weekend (September 2003) and PRoba Awards (December 2003). Public relations consultancies, public relations directors, managers in businesses and public relations buyers, marketing directors, state institutions, CEOs, national and international media, university lecturers and students were identified as the key audiences to be reached. The primary geographical area was Russia, but of equal importance was the requirement to demonstrate to an international audience that the Russian public relations sector was capable of taking positive action to change bad practice.

A series of conferences, debates and educational events was organized, including the PR Days in the Moscow Festival. The organizers of the festival were RPRA and SPN Granat, with support from IPRA, CERP and sponsors Philip Morris Sales and Marketing. Within the framework of the festival, an international conference, 'Public relations in the process of strengthening the reputation of Russia' took place. The forum was attended by more than 450 people from 5 countries and 18 Russian cities. Public relations specialists, business people, politicians, public figures from Russia, Germany, the UK, Egypt, the Baltic states and CIS countries took part. Influential speakers included Mikhail Gorbachev, Irina Khakamada, Vice-Speaker of the State Council of the Russian Federation Federal Assembly and Sergey Mironov, Chairman of the Council of Federation of the Federal Assembly of the Russian Federation. Seventy-nine mass media representatives covered the 2003 event, producing 65 published items and 7 TV reports.

Other events included The Baltic PR Weekend – 3rd International PR Conference and PRoba-2003, whose geographical coverage included 45 per cent of the north-west region, 28 per cent of the Central Federal Region, and 27 per cent of the Baltic and CIS countries. Media coverage included 40 print items, 60 online internet messages, 15 radio transmissions, all 3 Russian and 7 regional TV companies.

Evaluation outcomes

On 6 April 2004 a Partnership Agreement was made between the IPRA Golden World Award contest and the RPRA PRoba contest. Signed in St

Table 8.2   *Evaluation outcomes*

	PR Days in Moscow 2003	The Baltic PR Weekend 2003	PRoba Award 2003
Number of delegates/ entries	450	350	100
Breakdown of the target audiences:			
PR consultancies	105	85	10
Business structures: PR/marketing directors, CEOs, etc	128	114	48
State institutions	48	37	6
National and International media	79	42	2
University lecturers and students	81	68	31
General public	9	4	3

Petersburg, it was seen as another step towards bringing Russian public relations up to world-class standards. Growing understanding of how diverse audiences such as companies and organizations, government and interest groups, customers and investors, all require different approaches and different forms of dialogue, was being achieved. The role of effective and efficient internal communication was increasingly appreciated, and economic leaders started to care about their public image through sponsorship and charity work by promoting their companies as responsible corporate citizens. Learning from international best practice, Russian oil, gas, pulp-and-paper and steel companies are investing in environmental programmes and communicating these changes to industry and the general public.

Corporate social responsibility campaigning and growing trust in public relations agencies for the supply of such professional programmes, has increased the range of services offered by the Russian public relations industry, including financial, investor and analyst relations.

REFLECTION

Based on the information provided:

i.   How does this case illustrate the complex boundaries between public relations vs propaganda/communication vs information/power vs influence?

ii.   Is the RPRA likely to become increasingly dependent on rational or generative thinking of itself and of its' stakeholders?

iii.   Does the UNDP definition of ethical communication offer universal values?

iv.   Is the RPRA monistic, dualistic or pluralistic in its approach to governance?

v.   Do RPRA's evaluation outcomes suggest the transfer process is working well enough for the operational strategy to be sustained in the longer term?

Glossary

The following definitions used in this book are based on terminology generally accepted by public relations management teachers and practitioners in Europe and beyond.

aim   A combination of objective and goal, maybe both short and long term, sometimes involving hope and aspiration in an organizational mission statement

decision making   Part of the problem-solving cycle in campaigning, where choices are made between options and courses of action and which are subject to information analysis and behavioural outcomes

environment   Micro and macro economic, political, social, legal and technological organizational fields of influence that can impact on public relations strategy and performance

goal   A concrete, occasionally value-added objective often seen to be shorter term

information   Asymmetric messages which, by virtue of being one-way, are not, in social psychological terms, a valid communication process

intelligence   The collation of information such as competitive or security data, gathered and shared in a closed systems culture or network. Formerly, the term applied to news or information gathered and distributed openly

mission   The fundamental purpose of an organization which underpins its strategy and is produced as a public statement

objective   A bottom-line, measurable statement of what must be achieved, often seen to be longer term than 'goal'

policy   Formal and informal ground rules or operational criteria applied for purposes of decision making and quality control

PR   A media acronym for public relations as a profession/industry. Sometimes used to refer to a person/specialist, eg celebrity PR, but used interchangeably in this book

PRO   A managerial acronym for a public relations officer at junior/middle management level, usually located in-house and a qualified member of the Chartered Institute of Public Relations (CIPR). Pronounced by letter as an abbreviation and not as the prefix 'pro'

public relations practice   The process of earning understanding and support with the aim of influencing opinion and behaviour through planned and sustained efforts to establish and maintain goodwill between an organization and its interested parties

public relations theory   The discipline of university-led, specialist research and knowledge grounded in communication theory and empirically-based evidence over time. The body of literature centres on cultural perceptions of reputation management as a result of what organizations do and say – and what others say about them or the people that represent them

scenario   A future view of the organizational environment based on measurable perceptions of change and uncertainty

skills set   Tools and techniques accrued as a result of education, training and experience, often involving continuous professional development (CPD)

strategy   A dynamic means or process by which an organization aims to fulfil its vision and mission statements

tactic Decisions and actions intended to achieve short-term objectives, which can be proactive or reactive

vision A written concept based on a function (task) or view (idea) of an organization's future aims

Bibliography

Barrass, R (2002) *Scientists Must Write*, Routledge, London

Barrett, D J (2004) A best practice approach to designing a change management programme, Ch. 2, Part I in S Oliver, *Handbook of Corporate Communication and Public Relations: Pure and Applied*, Routledge, London

Baskin, O, Aronoff, C and Lattimore, D (1997) *Public Relations*, 4th edn, Brown & Benchmark, Madison, WI

Bennett, R (1996) *Corporate Strategy & Business Planning*, Pitman, London

Berger, B K and Reber B H (2006) *Gaining Influence in Public Relations: the role of resistance in practice*, Lawrence Erlbaum, New Haven

Bernstein, D (1991) *Company Image and Reality*, Cassell, London

Boje, D M (2001) *Narrative Methods for Organisational and Communication Research*, Sage, London

Boorstin, D (1963) *The Image or What Happened to the American Dream*, Penguin, Harmondsworth

Botan, C H and Hazleton, V (eds) (2006) *Public Relations Theory II*, Lawrence Erlbaum, New Haven

Boulding, E (1956) *The Image*, The University of Michigan Press, Ann Arbor, MI

Braam, G J M and Nijssen, E J (2004) Performance effects of using the balanced score card: a note on the Dutch experience, in *Long Range Planning*, **37**, 4, August, Elsevier, Oxford

Brooking, A (1996) *Intellectual Capital/Core asset for the third millennium enterprise*, Thompson Business, London

Broom, G M and Dozier, D M (eds) (1990) *Using Research in Public Relations*, Prentice Hall, Harlow

Brouthers, K D (1995) Strategic alliances: choose your partners, *Long Range Planning*, **28**, 3, pp 18–25

Bryman, A (2004) *Social Research Methods*, 2nd edn, Oxford University Press, Oxford

Chesborough, H W and Teece, D J (1996) When is virtual virtuous: organizing for innovation, *Harvard Business Review*, January-February

Christians, C and Traeber, M (1997) *Communication Ethics and Universal Values*, Sage, London

Christopher, M, Payne, A and Ballantyne, D (1994) *Relationship Marketing*, Butterworth-Heinemann, Oxford

CIPR/MORI/Business in the Community (2002) *Reputation and the bottom line*, CIPR, London

Cornelissen, J (2004) *Corporate Communications Theory and Practice*, Sage, London

Crane, A and Matten, D (2004) *Business Ethics: A European Perspective*, Oxford University Press, Oxford

Cravens, D W (1994) *Strategic Marketing*, 4th edn, Irwin, Toronto

Crossman, A and McIlwee, T (1995) *Signalling Discontent: A study of the 1994 signal workers' dispute*, Thames Valley University School of Management, London

de Wit, B and Meyer, R (1999) *Strategy Synthesis: resolving strategy paradoxes to create competitive advantage*, Thompson Learning, London

Dowling, C (1993) Developing your company image into a corporate asset, *Long Range Planning*, **26**, pp 101–9

Ehling, W P (1985) Application of decision theory in the construction of a theory of public relations management, II, *Public Relations Research and Education*, **2**, 1, pp 4–22, in Broom, G M and Dozier, D M (eds) *Using Research in Public Relations*, Prentice Hall, Harlow

Elliott, F (1975) *A Dictionary of Politics*, Penguin, Harmondsworth

Engler, P (1992) Building transnational alliances to create competitive advantage, *Long Range Planning*, **25**, 1

Ewing, M T, Caruana, A and Loy, E R (1999) Corporate reputation and perceived risk in professional engineering services, *Corporate Communication International Journal*, **4**, 3, pp 121–8

Fryxell, G E and Wang, J (1994) The Fortune's Corporate Reputation Index: Reputation of what?, *Journal of Management*, **20**, 1, pp 1–14

Gorb, P (1992) The psychology of corporate identity, *European Management Journal*, **10**, p 310

Grant, A W H and Schlesinger, L A (1995) Realize your customer's full profit potential, *Harvard Business Review*, September-October, pp 59–72

Gregerson, H B, Morrison, A J and Black, J S (1999) Leaders for the Global Frontier, *Frontline 21*, **21**, 4, International Public Relations Association (IPRA), Dorking

Grunig, J E (ed) (1992) *Excellence in Public Relations and Communication Management*, Lawrence Erlbaum, New Jersey

Grunig, J E and Hunt, T (1984) *Managing Public Relations*, Holt, Rinehart & Winston, Austin, TX

Grunig, J E and White, J (1992) The effect of world views on public relations theory and practice, in Grunig, JE (1992) *Excellence in Public Relations and Communication Management*, Lawrence Erlbaum, New Jersey

Grunig, L A, Grunig, J E and Dozier, D M (2002) *Organisations: A study in three countries*, Lawrence Erlbaum, New Jersey

Gugler, P (1992) Building transnational alliances to create competitive advantage, *Long Range Planning*, **25**, 1, pp 90–99

Guiltinan, J P and Paul, G W (1994) *Marketing Management: Strategies and programmes*, 5th edn, McGraw-Hill, Maidenhead

Hayes, A F (2005) *Statistical Methods for Communication Science*, Lawrence Erlbaum, New Haven

Hearit, K (2006) *Crisis Management by Apology: corporate response to alligations of wrongdoing*, Lawrence Erlbaum, New Haven

Houlden, B (1988) The corporate conscience, *Management Today*, August

Illegems, V and Verbeke, A (2004) Telework: what does it mean for management? *Long Range Planning?*, **37**, 4

Ind, N (1997) *The Corporate Brand*, Macmillan Business Press, London

Jefkins, F (1993) *Planned Press and Public Relations*, Blackie Academic and Professional, London

Jobber, D (1995) *Principles and Practice of Marketing*, McGraw-Hill, Maidenhead

Johnson, G and Scholes, K (1993) *Exploring Corporate Strategy*, 3rd edn, Prentice Hall, Harlow

Johnson, G and Scholes, K (2002) *Exploring Corporate Strategy*, 6th edn, Prentice Hall, Harlow

Jolly, V (1996) Global strategies in the 1990s, *Mastering Management Series* no 5, *Financial Times*, London

Kaid, L L (ed) (2004) *Handbook of Political Communication Research*, Lawrence Erlbaum, New Haven

Kaplan, R S and Norton, D P (2001) The Strategy-Focused Organization, Harvard Business School Press, Boston, MA

Kirban, L and Jackson, B C (1990) Using research to plan programmes, Chapter 2 in eds G M Broom and D M Dozier, *Using Research in Public Relations*, Prentice Hall, Harlow

Koter, P and Mirdak, W (1978) Marketing and Public Relations, *Journal of Marketing*, **42**, 4, pp13–20

Kotler, P (1988) *Marketing Management: Analysis, Planning, Implementation and Control*, Prentice Hall, Harlow

Kotler, P (1994) *Marketing Management: Analysis, Planning, Implementation and Control*, 8th edn, Prentice Hall, Harlow

Kotler, P, Armstrong, G, Saunders, J and Wong, V (1999) *Principles of Marketing*, 2nd European edition, Prentice Hall, Harlow

Lerbinger, O (2006) *Interacting with Interest Groups, Media and Governments*, Lawrence Erlbaum, New Haven

Lerbinger, O and Sullivan, A J (1965) *Information, Influence and Communication*, Basic Books, New York

L'Etang, J and Pieczka, M (2006) *Public Relations: critical debates and contemporary practice*, Lawrence Erlbaum, New Haven

Luftman, J N *et al* (2004) *Managing the Information Technology Resource: Leadership in the Information Age*, Pearson Prentice Hall, Harlow

Lynch, K (1991) *The Image of the City*, The MIT Press, Cambridge, MA

Maathuis, O J M (1993) *Corporate Image, Performance and Communication*, Eburon, Delft

Mackiewicz, A (1993) *Guide to Building a Global Image*, McGraw-Hill, Maidenhead

Macrae, C (1991) *World Class Brands*, Addison-Wesley, London

Mayer, M (1961) *Maddison Avenue*, Penguin, Harmondsworth

McMaster, M (1996) Foresight: Exploring the structure of the future, *Long-Range Planning*, **29**, 2, pp 149–55, April

McQuail, D (1994) *Mass Communication Theory*, Sage, London

Mintzberg, H and Quinn, J B (eds) (1996) *The Strategy Process: Concepts, contexts, cases*, 3rd edn, Prentice Hall, Harlow

Mintzberg, H, Ahlstrand, B and Lampel, J (1998) *Strategy Safari: A guided tour through the wilds of strategic management*, The Free Press, New York

Morgan, G (1997) *Images of Organization*, Sage, London

Mozammel, M and Odugbemi, S (eds) (2005) *With the Support of Multitudes, Information and Communication for Development*, DFID/Development Communication Division, External Affairs, The World Bank, New York

Newman, W (1956) Basic objectives which shape the character of a company, *The Journal of Business*, **26,** p 211

O'Sullivan, T, Hartley, J, Saunders, D, Montgomery, M and Fiske, J (1994) *Key Concepts in Communication and Cultural Studies*, Routledge, London

Oliver, S (1997) *Corporate Communication: Principles, Techniques and Strategies*, Kogan Page, London

Oliver, S (1998) Technology Assisted Teaching and Learning: Design implications for communication courses on the internet, *Journal of Communication Management*, **3**, 1

Oliver, S (2000a) Message from the CEO: a three minute rule? *Corporate Communication: An International Journal*, **5**, 3

Oliver, S (2000b) Symmetrical Communication: Does reality support rhetoric? *Corporate Communication: An International Journal*, **15**, 1

Oliver, S (2001) *Public Relations Strategy*, Kogan Page, London

Oliver, S (2002) A crisis of confidence: M&S plc, in (eds) D Moss and B De Santo, *Public Relations Cases: International Perspectives*, Routledge, London

Oliver, S (2004) Communicating a continuity plan: The action stations framework, in S Oliver, Ch 18, *Handbook of Corporate Communication and Public Relations: Pure and Applied*, Routledge, London

Pearce, J A II and Robinson, R B Jr (1982) *Strategic Management: Strategy Formulation and Implementation*, Irwin

Petrash, G (1996) Dow's journey to a knowledge value management culture, *European Management Journal*, **14**, 4, pp 365–73

Pickton, D and Broderick, A (2005) *Integrated Marketing Communications*, 2nd edn, Pearson Education Ltd, Harlow

Porter, M (1985) *Competitive Advantage*, Free Press, New York

Quinn, J B *et al* (1996) Managing professional intellect: making the most of the best, *Harvard Business Review*, March-April, pp 71–80

Reich, R B (1990) Who is us?, *Harvard Business Review*, January-February

Singer, P (1993) *Practical Ethics*, Cambridge University Press, Cambridge

Smith, A and O'Neill, G (1997) Seamless marketing communications, in *CBI Corporate Communication Handbook*, Kogan Page, London

Stacey, R D (1991) *The Chaos Frontier: Creative strategic control for business*, Butterworth-Heinemann, Oxford

Stacey, R D (1993) *Strategic Management and Organisational Dynamics*, Pitman, London

Stacks, D W (2002) *Primer of Public Relations Research*, The Guilford Press, Hove

Stanley, J (1991) Market Communications: How Marks and Spencer does it, *European Management Journal*, **9**, pp 329–33

Stuart, H (1999) Towards a definitive model of the corporate identity management, *Corporate Communication International Journal*, **4**, 4, pp 200–7

Thompson, J L (1995) *Strategy in Action*, Chapman & Hall, London

Toffler, A (1970) *Future Shock: a study of mass bewilderment in the face of accelerating change*, Bodley Head, London

Toth, E L (ed) (2006) *The Future of Excellence in Public Relations and Communication Management: challenges for the next generation*, Lawrence Erlbaum, New Haven

van den Bosch, A L M, de Jong, M D and Elving, W J L (2005) How corporate visual identity supports reputation, *Corporate Communication: An International Journal*, **10**, 2, p 108

Van Riel, C B M (1995) *Principles of Corporate Communication*, Prentice Hall, Harlow

Walker, J, Holloway, I and Wheeler, S (2005) *Research Ethics Review*, **1**, 3, p 92

Weintraub, A E and Pinkleton, B E (2006) *Planning and Managing Effective Communication Programs*, 2nd edn, Lawrence Erlbaum, New Haven

White, C (2004) *Strategic Management*, Palgrave Macmillan, London

White, J and Dozier, D M (1992) Public Relations and Management Decision Making, in Grunig, J E (ed) *Excellence in Public Relations and Communication Management*, Lawrence Erlbaum, New Jersey

Wines, W A (2006) *Ethics, Law and Business*, Lawrence Erlbaum, New Haven

Further reading

Alsop R J (2004) *The 18 Immutable Laws of Corporate Reputation*, Kogan Page, London

Bovee C L, Thill J V and Schatzman B E (2003) *Business Communication Today*, 7th edn, Prentice Hall Pearson Education International, Harlow

Clampitt P G (2001) *Communicating for Managerial Effectiveness*, 2nd Ed., Sage, London

Clowe KE and Baack D (2004) *Integrated Advertising, Promotion & Marketing Communications*, 2nd edn, Pearson Prentice Hall, Harlow

Davidson H (2005) *The Committed Enterprise*, 2nd edn, Elsevier

Davis A (2002) *Public Relations Democracy*, Manchester University Press, Manchester

Davis A (2004) *Mastering Public Relations*, Palgrave Macmillan, Basing stoke

Fernandez J (2004) *Corporate Communications*, Sage, London

Fill C (2006) *Marketing Communication*, 4th edn, FT Prentice Hall, Harlow

Goudge P (2006) *Employee Research*, Kogan Page, London

Greenwood J (2005) *Essential Law for Journalists*, 18th edn, Oxford University Press, Oxford

Hannigan T (2005) *Management Concepts and Practices*, 4th edn, FT Prentice Hall, Harlow

Hannington T (2004) *How to Measure and Manage Your Corporate Reputation*, Gower, Aldershot

Hargie O, (ed) (2006) *The Handbook of Communication Skills*, 3rd edn, Routledge, Oxford

Holman D and Thorpe R (2003) *Management & Language*, Sage, London

Jessup L and Valacich (2006) *Information Systems Today: Why IS Matters*, 2nd edn, Pearson Prentice Hall, Harlow

Krajewski LJ and Ritzman LP (2002) *Operations Management: Strategy & Analysis*, 6th edn, Prentice Hall, Harlow

McKenzie J and van Winkelen C (2004) *Understanding the Knowledge Organization*, Thomson, London

Meijer M-M (2004) *Does Success Breed Success? Effects of news and advertising on corporate reputation*, Aksant, Amsterdam

Orna E (2004) *Information in Strategy and Practice*, Gower, Aldershot

Pettinger R (2004) *Contemporary Strategic Management*, Palgrave Macmillan, Basingstoke

Price A (2004) *Human Resource Management in a Business Context*, 2nd edn, Thomson, London

Quinn R E, Faerman S R, Thompson M P and McGrath M R (2003) *Becoming a Master Manager:A Competency Framework*, 3rd edn, Wiley, Chichester

Robbins S P and Decenzo D A (2004) *Fundamentals of Management*, 4th edn, Pearson Prentice Hall, Harlow

Sanghi S (2004) *The Handbook of Competency Mapping*, Sage, London

Sjöstrand S-E, Sandberg J and Tyrstrup M (2001) *Invisible Management: The Social Construction of Leadership*, Thomson Learning, London

Soloman MR, Marshall GW and Stuart EW (2006) *Marketing: Real People, Real Choices*, 4th edn, Pearson Prentice Hall, Harlow

Swart J, Mann C, Brown S & Price A (2005) *Human Resource Development*, Elsevier Butterworth Heinemann

Whittington R (2001) *What is Strategy – and does it matter?*, Thomson Learning, London

Index

NB: page numbers in *italic* indicate figures or tables